Anonymous

A Letter addressed to His Majesty's Attorney General and Solicitor General

In which the Doctrines lately maintained in Parliament, on the Subject of voluntary Subscriptions, are considered

Anonymous

A Letter addressed to His Majesty's Attorney General and Solicitor General
In which the Doctrines lately maintained in Parliament, on the Subject of voluntary Subscriptions, are considered

ISBN/EAN: 9783337106942

Printed in Europe, USA, Canada, Australia, Japan

Cover: Foto ©ninafisch / pixelio.de

More available books at **www.hansebooks.com**

A LETTER

ADDRESSED TO

HIS MAJESTY's

ATTORNEY GENERAL and SOLICITOR GENERAL,

IN WHICH

THE DOCTRINES LATELY MAINTAINED IN PARLIAMENT,

ON THE SUBJECT OF

VOLUNTARY SUBSCRIPTIONS,

ARE CONSIDERED.

LONDON:

PRINTED FOR J. DEBRETT, OPPOSITE BURLINGTON-HOUSE, PICCADILLY.

M,DCC,XCIV.

A

LETTER

TO THE

ATTORNEY AND SOLICITOR GENERAL.

GENTLEMEN,

WHEN the question which is the subject of discussion in the following sheets was first started, I could not imagine that an opportunity would have been given to private individuals to enter into any controversy about it. Its magnitude appeared to me in a peculiar manner not only to entitle it to parliamentary investigation, but also to require a complete parliamentary decision. Had our Legislators thought proper to decide this point even in a way that might in future affect our liberties, as their act; I should, probably, have felt it to be my *present* duty, as an individual, to submit to this *legitimate* expression of their will: but as it has been judged expedient to leave this question still in suspense, I trust, that without deviating from that respect which is always due to the opinions of the Legiflature, I may be now permitted to enter at large upon the difcuffion: and as I may alfo be allowed fairly to conclude that their deliberation has been influenced by the advice which you have given, for it does not appear that any other *eminent legal* characters in either houfe have given to this meafure the fanction of their fentiments, I know not to whom I can with equal propriety addrefs the following pages, as to yourfelves; to you, Gentlemen, who, holding high and refponfible fituations under the crown, have advanced to fupport this queftion of Subfcriptions, as confiftent with the fpirit of our conftitution, and fanctioned by the practice of our laws. To you, under fuch circumftances, no further apology for a public comment on your conduct can be neceffary; and where the caufe is itfelf of the higheft conftitutional importance, where the object of animadverfion is nothing lefs than an open attempt to defend a violation of the fundamental principles of conftitutional juftice, an effort to expofe fophiftry, and to defend our liberties, requires none with the public, though the execution may be not equal to the magnitude of the fubject.

I cannot but feel the utmoft fatisfaction in contemplating the characters, with whom it is my fate at prefent to contend. The unimpeachable

integrity

integrity of private life, while it presumes the influence of similar principles in a public career, excludes the suspicion of personal attack; and, at the same time, that it affords an excuse for the maintenance of erroneous doctrines upon the ground of misinformation, relieves the mind from the painful task of making any odious charge. With such characters, a fair discussion may be expected, and reason and justice may for once hope to triumph, through the means of candour, over prejudice, ignorance, and self-interest. At the same time, though I am far from wishing to degrade that profession for which I am myself designed, and to which I shall think it an honour one day to belong, yet I cannot but lament, that upon such great points of policy and constitution, the legislature should yield so much to the direction of professional men; for I must confess, that upon the evidence of history, my mind is impressed with a strong conviction, that, generally speaking, the lawyers are not the men most calculated to decide upon such questions. They have in all times been but too prone to derive their political ideas from the same confined source from whence they draw their legal notions. They may hunt a question of law through the several books of the profession, but they must not attempt to reduce to the minute precision, and within the strict bounds of law precedents,

cases

cafes often times arifing out of paffions, which will fcarce admit of any reftraint at all. They expect on all occafions to direct the prefent, after the example of the paft; without making any allowance for thofe changes of circumftance which may poffibly have deftroyed all that analogy upon which fuch arguments muft be founded. They appear either to forget, or to difregard, a diftinction of which I can never lofe fight, between the conftitution and the law. The firft laying down *general principles* applicable to every emergency, and giving all that latitude which the extremeft cafe can require, confiftent with national fecurity; the latter, impofing rules for particular cafes, to which cafes alone thofe rules can in ftrict conftruction be applied. Inftead of arguing upon the great ground of conftitutional principle, which is capable of embracing every fubject, they refort to a too frequently ftrained conftruction of law, and truft to the affiftance of precedents for the fupport of their tottering fabric.

In ordinary judicial queftions, whether civil or criminal, which arife between man and man, the law cannot be too ftrictly obferved; and its conftruction cannot be better afcertained, than by the precedents of cafes which have been already decided by it. The perfection of civil liberty depends upon the rule of conduct prefcribed for

each

each member of the community being exactly defined; and that general good order and happy security, which is the natural result of well defined law, amply compensates for any temporary or individual inconvenience which may accidentally arise, out of what, in some instances, might be called an excessive severity of restriction. But when the subject of discussion is some political point, some constitutional question, the field of argument becomes more extensive, the rule of conduct is less defined, involves a greater variety of circumstances, and consequently renders the means of decision apparently more complicated. The state of the times forms the most important part of the consideration of such questions, and of itself renders the application of precedents in such cases always difficult, often times impossible. It is easy to calculate the capacity of a man, and as easy to guard against the evils his conduct may produce; and to proportion the force of prevention to the gradation of danger; but national events, their causes and their consequences, being on some occasions alike incalculable by human foresight, are equally beyond the reach of the provisions of human wisdom. Acting upon such a consciousness of human imperfection, the constitution of England regulates upon general principles what shall be the conduct observed by its government, al-

lowing

lowing to itself the exercise of mercy, whenever the executive power shall exceed the limits of its authority upon the ground of *notorious* and *great* necessity. When the crown, upon reasonable grounds, exercises any prerogative with which it is not constitutionally entrusted, the tendency of a bill of indemnity is not to constitute a precedent by *legalizing* the measure, but, on the contrary, by granting a pardon to that particular case, declares it by a necessary implication to be illegal, and consequently not fit to be drawn forth as an example for the future. The truth is, that in all those extreme cases in which the crown may without hazard to itself exercise an *extreme* power, its justification does not at all depend upon the analogy of precedents. If the necessity of the times does not present a sufficient excuse of itself, the mere similarity of previous cases can avail but little. Who will dare to act on precedents of tyranny? Yet who will affirm, that no such precedents are to be found in our history?

On the present occasion, however strong my opinion may be against the measure itself of raising money by subscription, it is not my intention *now* either to question its policy, to arraign the wisdom of the invention, or to dispute its salutary tendency; my object is infinitely more important; it is to *insist*, that *whatever* may be
the

the advantages to be derived from the adoption of *any plan*, that plan *must*, nevertheless, be consistent with the spirit of our constitution, and the manner of its execution consonant to the mode prescribed by the standing law of the land. In the case now under consideration, I affirm, that the conduct of the king's ministers has been unconstitutional and illegal. The question now is, not what we shall pay; but on what authority we shall pay any thing? The necessity of supply is not contended; but it is the system by which that supply shall be raised, to which we object. In short, it is the revival of the old question, concerning which the contest, and the issue of that contest, must be acknowledged to comprehend the most melancholy, though perhaps the most interesting period of English history. It is nothing less in point of fact, than an attempt to raise money on the subject without the previous concurrence of the legislature, constitutionally expressed by an act of parliament. It is the first step towards reviving the odious doctrine of extra-parliamentary taxation; an attempt which *no necessity* can justify.

I have observed, that in several debates and parliamentary conversations, which have lately taken place relative to this subject, many broad assertions have been made, to which various qualifications and provisoes have been afterwards annexed.

pexed. The discussion by others again has been deprecated in toto, as involving an abstract question, the decision of which could have no reference to the present point. I can discover no motive for such a conduct, but that which springs from an inclination to bewilder and perplex; by which means the public may be liable to be blinded as to the real question, and wholly lose sight of the great interest which they have in its final decision: and there was the greater necessity for the exertion of every various artifice to effect this purpose, because it is impossible to conceive any question more simple, or one which arises more naturally, out of a fact equally simple and incontestible. The fact is, that the minister of the crown has in his ministerial capacity, without the previous authority of parliament, issued letters to the lord lieutenants of different counties, calling upon them to solicit and to receive the voluntary contributions of those persons who shall be willing to subscribe, for the purpose of defraying the expences incident to an additional system of internal defence. The question which arises on this fact is, simply, whether such letters having been issued without the previous authority of parliament, have, or have not, been issued according to law? That is, in order to make the question yet more pointed, can the crown, by any device, *move* its subjects to a voluntary

tary contribution towards defraying the expences of the government, without previously obtaining a parliamentary sanction? It is conceived, that no such device can at this time be practised without a gross violation of the principles established in our constitution, without an actual infringement of an *existing* statute, and without being wholly unsupported by any precedent whatever.

Precedents being in fact only the recital of past transactions, can derive no weight from any intrinsic property in themselves; their force depends entirely upon the authority from whence they proceed, and must be wholly comparative. In points of law, precedents which are founded on the opinion of one judge, may often carry far greater weight with them than those which are built on the opinion of another. A precedent established by the decision of a court of justice, is yet more conclusive; but every other species of precedent must yield to the irresistible force of one established by an act of parliament. Such is the nature of precedents applying to points of law, and admitting of a stability of decision, which in political questions is utterly impracticable. The law is always the same, but the times are continually changing. That which is law to day, unless overturned by some competent authority, must also to-morrow

morrow direct the conduct of those who are subject to it; but that which in policy is at this moment strictly expedient, may, perhaps in the next, become absolutely improper. The event of a battle, or an unexpected turn in a negotiation, may produce circumstances uncalculated, and for which no provision had been made; but, above all, a revolution in the opinions and dispositions of mankind, may subvert at once the whole political scheme, or make ruin the inevitable consequence of perseverance. Perhaps, if there ever was a period in history compleatly illustrative of this position, it is the present, when the ideas of men are preparing to flow in new channels, and to direct their pursuits to new objects; when the human mind appears for a moment to have suspended its functions from a dread of slavery on the one hand, and from the fear of anarchy on the other; it is as it were an awful crisis, big with the fate of posterity; a sort of chaos, awaiting the hand of some skilful artist to mould it into shape, and to create the happiness of mankind. At such a period, refinement in conduct appears only the effect of insanity: to expect ultimately to delude men out of rational rights, is a folly to be exceeded only by attempting it. The deception, when the veil is drawn aside, is calculated only to exasperate, and to *fix* the wavering

wavering refolution. The only path to be purfued, is that which plain common fenfe directs, to harmonize and to conciliate. To feek for, and to apply then to times which are without example in hiftory, precedents in themfelves hoftile to liberty, and which have arifen in periods unmarked by any extraordinary events, is fomething worfe than ridiculous; and to expect at fuch a moment to enforce unrefifted the doctrines propofed to be eftablifhed, is an excefs of folly which is only to be regretted from the confequences it is finally calculated to produce among the unoffending innocent multitude. But even granting that every cafe which has been cited, is a cafe in point, what has been your conduct on this occafion? You have been fighting the weakeft againft the ftrongeft point; you have been upholding the force of a variety of precedents, founded on mere opinions of judges, againft the exprefs declaration of an act of parliament. Such a conduct appears to me to amount to nothing lefs than maintaining, that, upon the authority of judicial proceedings, the operation of an act of parliament may be fufpended; and that not only a court of juftice, but any one of the judges of that court, provided he has eftablifhed a high legal character, may affume a power of legiflation. To argue either the abfurdity, or the rafhnefs of fuch a doctrine, would be to

infult

insult the understandings of the people. It is a point which cannot be established, but by the total subversion of the constitution of this country.

Considering all precedents on constitutional questions in the light I do; refering every thing to principles, and not to examples; accommodating those principles to the times; and conceiving every period to be entitled to make its own example according to present exigency; I should have scarcely felt it incumbent on me to animadvert, in any degree, upon those precedents which have been advanced, had they been only *incidentally* introduced into those defences of administration upon which the parliament appears to have founded its late decision; but when I reflect that these precedents do in fact constitute the *whole* foundation on which those arguments have been raised, the tendency of which has been to weaken the authority of an existing act of parliament; I should reflect, that I had been wanting in that justice which is due to the subject, had I neglected the opportunity of annihilating, in the first instance, the whole ground of defence, by examining the applicability of the precedents themselves.

The first name which appears in your catalogue of authorities, is Lord Coke; and his opinion, as collected from his 12th Report, if indeed it may be be ranked as a precedent, is confidered as decidedly in favour of voluntary benevolences. Allowing to thefe opinions all the authority of law at the time when they were given, ftill they can have no force now, if the 13 C. 2. is not repealed; but even waiving that act, there is ftill fome ground for difputing the authority of Lord Coke, to the extent required, and that ground is furnifhed by himfelf. I have here one obfervation to introduce, which is, perhaps, of fome importance to the public, as it may poffibly affift them in forming a judgment on this fubject; —it is, that the 12th Report of Lord Coke is wholly compofed from a collection of loofe papers, and which, in many inftances, and particularly in the prefent, feem to have been intended merely as memorandums, probably preparatory to fome future defign. The utmoft extent to which any opinion delivered in this report, can be ftrained, confiftent with thofe contained in his other works, is, that the king was not prohibited by any ftatute, from receiving the voluntary fubfcription of a fingle individual. And what he does affert, he deduces as a confequence from the ftatute 11 Hen. 7. c. 10. It does not appear upon a view of this ftatute, that any other inference can be drawn from it, in favour of *voluntary* fubfcriptions, than what I have mentioned; and it affords very ftrong evidence, that the crown had

no

no means of compelling any payment, where the demand originated from itself; since this act is intended to give him a power of forcing the payment of those sums which had been subscribed, though not paid in, by the *voluntary* and *free will* of his subjects; and the necessity of such an act, (for we must presume no act to be passed without some necessity) is conclusive, that he did not possess even such an inferior prerogative, as that of forcing a subject to fulfil a voluntary promise.

It is observable also, that the preamble to this statute states, that " Divers of his Majesty's sub-
" jects had *severally* granted divers sums of
" money of their free wills and benevolence*."
This word *severally*, if it has any meaning, must intend the subscriptions of individuals singly, and *not associated together in bodies*; such as is the case at present; and as it was in a case of the reign of Ed. 3. on which I shall hereafter enlarge; and in stating which case Lord Coke, in that which is perhaps the most perfect of all his works, his commentary on Magna Charta, contained in his 2d Institute, declares, that it was finally conceded that " *no such grants should be made but by parlia-*
" *ment*†."

The next authority which you have adduced

---

* App. (R.)   † 2 Inst. 60.

as tending to legalize the prefent fyftem of *exciting* voluntary contributions, is a parenthetical opinion delivered by Lord Hardwicke, in pronouncing fentence on the rebel peers, in 1746, and which profeffes to declare the fubfcriptions of that time neither unconftitutional nor illegal. It is to be obferved, that this opinion of Lord Hardwicke was totally extrajudicial, as it arofe upon no point which was before him for decifion; it was given incidentally in the courfe of an eulogy on the zeal and fpirit of the Englifh people, when there could be no reafon to quarrel with the mode of exertion, from the nature of the cafe; and even if there had been, when few perfons would have dared to find fault; but when on the contrary there was rather a general tendency to magnify into virtue, what in effect proceeded from neceffity. It was rather an opinion which originated in the momentary enthufiafm of the judge's mind, without being founded on any conviction, the refult of deep and laborious reflection. It was given from the feat of juftice; but it has no pretenfion to the weight of judicial authority. Yet, even allowing to this opinion all the force which the authority of that great lawyer can give to it, let us look a little into the circumftances attending the meafure. Thefe fubfcriptions were made with a view to encreafe the ftrength of the kingdom, at a moment of

open,

open, and at that time fuccefsful, rebellion, and at a moment when the rebels were advancing by hafty marches to the metropolis. It was at that particular, *punctum temporis belli*, that period which juftifies the fufpending the courfe of juftice, which authorizes the temporary fhutting of the courts of law, which legalizes every exertion of every defcription, not merely by the authority of conftitutional law, not by the power of an act of parliament, but by the paramount law of extreme neceffity. Such was the cafe to which thofe fubfcriptions were pointed, and to the legality of which Lord Hardwicke adverted: but this maxim can have no weight in any cafe fhort of that extreme one, which gave rife to the queftion of that day. In every cafe of urgency fhort of this, the rule of conduct for the executive magiftrate is diftinctly laid down; in that which feems to approach the neareft to fuch a cafe, namely, when there is ground to apprehend an invafion, or even when an infurrection has actually commenced, a certain line is prefcribed to the fovereign. In fuch an emergency he is permitted to call out the militia; but even when he has done that, he muft affemble the parliament within fourteen days, that they may be enabled to judge of the neceffity, and prevent the mifchief of the meafure, if the neceffity does not exift. Upon what principle of reafon then is it poffible that

the

the crown can be permitted, in this prefent inftance, to take any ftep towards raifing not only men but *money*, without the confent of parliament, when in a cafe of at leaft equal emergency, it is not allowed by the exprefs direction of a ftatute to affemble *that force which already exifts*, without at the fame time convening the parliament, which may be immediately enabled to fanction the meafure by its approbation? Upon this precedent I have only to remark, that in my humble opinion, the fituation of the country is at prefent fo widely different from what it was at the period alluded to by Lord Hardwicke, as to deftroy all analogy between the *circumftances* of the refpective times, and confequently to render the application of one cafe as an example for the other, *utterly impracticable*. But there is ftill another fundamental point which diftinguifhes this precedent from the prefent cafe;—in the firft, the fubfcription was *purely voluntary*; in the latter, it *has originated* in a *motion from the crown*; and this diftinction is alone fufficient to overturn all reafoning founded on the analogy of the two cafes.

It is fingular, that pending the prefent queftion, this point fhould have been accurately afcertained by one of the *zealous* advocates of adminiftration, who attempts to add the authority of Judge Forfter, to thofe which have been already cited

in favour of this meafure. He tells us "that
"on the 11th of October 1745, Sir Michael
"Forfter, then Recorder of Briftol, met at the
"Guildhall William Barnes, Efq. the then
"Mayor, the Aldermen, the other Members of
"the Corporation, and a very great number of
"the principal inhabitants, when a letter from
"his Grace the Duke of Newcaftle, then one of
"his Majefty's Principal Secretaries of State,
"was publicly read, *authorizing the magiftrates*
"(as from his Majefty) *to call the city to arms,*
"and to martial them into troops or companies
"*at their difcretion,* as alfo *for them to appoint*
"proper officers to the refpective corps; which
"letter was no fooner read, than an affociation
"was entered into for the fupport of the com-
"mon caufe, when the Mayor fubfcribed
"10,000l. in the name of the Chamber;" to
which it appears, that various other fubfcriptions were added by other public bodies and
individuals, within the city of Briftol.

Had this perfon, who is, I take for granted, accurate in his account of what was done in 1745 in his own city, been in any degree con-verfant either with the conftitution, or the law of his country, he would have known that what was done by the minifter of the crown at that time, was ftrictly conftitutional and legal; at that inftant of *open rebellion,* it was the *duty* of
the

the crown not to call upon the subject for a *guinea to buy a musket*, but to require the attendance of the subject himself with a musket upon his shoulder; and it should seem that this distinction was perfectly understood by the Duke of Newcastle, who, it is well known, acted always with Lord Harwicke at his right hand. He does not call upon the opulent city of Bristol for a *subscription*, but he *authorizes* the *magistrates to call the city to arms*; he calls upon the inhabitants of Bristol to do that, which on such an occasion every inhabitant of the country is bound to do on a requisition from the crown, and leaves to them to *martial themselves into troops at their own discretion, and to appoint their own officers*. In consequence of which *legal* requisition, the citizens of Bristol raise among themselves a subscription; not to be applied to *any purpose at the will of the crown*, but in order to enable themselves to do that which they were all *individually* bound to do, when required, viz. *to attend in person* their sovereign, at a moment of actual rebellion *within* the realm, for the defence of their constitution, their laws, their property, their country, and their king. Such was the subscription approved by Judge Forster, and such were those subscriptions to which Lord Hardwicke adverted as being strictly legal, as in truth they were; though, even on that occafion, there were perfons who felt fomething like prophetic fear, leaft thefe innocent, nay laudable efforts, fhould ferve as future examples, when a fimilar neceffity might not exift. The true diftinction is, that there are times in which the crown has a right of itfelf to command the perfonal attendance of all its fubjects, but *none* in which it can conftitutionally accept the *fubftitution* of their purfes.

With regard to the precedent of 1759, it appears upon the face of it, to have been a mere voluntary fubfcription for encreafing the levy money already voted by parliament. Upon this I need not at all expatiate; and the lefs, becaufe in confidering this queftion in a conftitutional light, I fhall have occafion to ftate a cafe of the fame kind.

The next in order is the precedent of 1778[*]. Early in that year (16th of January) the city of London, on the motion of fome of the principal merchants, affembled in common council for the purpofe of confidering of the means of raifing money among themfelves, in order to affift in defraying the expences of the war, or to raife new bodies of troops. A propofition to fuch an effect was made; which, after having been debated, was rejected. It would be highly indecent

[*] Vide Annual Regifter.

decent to pass this period of the argument; without doing that justice to the consistent and constitutional spirit of the citizens of London, which is so eminently due to their uniform zeal for the interests of their country, and their steady attachment to constitutional principles. It is a sufficient encomium on that respectable body to say of them, that on proper occasions, and when called upon in a *proper manner*, their loyal exertions are not to be exceeded; but whenever they feel the summons to be a violation of the constitution, no party clamour can prevent them from marking, by their conduct, their disapprobation of the measure. In consequence of this disappointment, those who had promoted the measure agreed again to meet, and accordingly did so at the London Tavern, from whence they published in the newspapers the following advertisement, dated January 17, 1778.

" At a meeting of several merchants and others,
" friends to their King and Country, in order to
" support the constitutional authority of Great
" Britain over her rebellious colonies in America,
" it was unanimously resolved and agreed, that a
" voluntary subscription be opened for the above
" purpose, and that the money arising there-
" from be applied, under the direction of a com-
" mittee of the subscribers, in raising men for
his

" his Majefty's fervice, in fuch manner as his Majefty in his wifdom fhall think fit."

And this was accompanied by offers from different perfons and places to raife corps of troops, which offers were accepted by the crown without even any fubfequent attempt to obtain the fanction of the legiflature.

At the time of the abovementioned meeting parliament was not fitting, but it met on the 20th; and the houfe of lords adjourned, after hearing the titles of feveral papers read, to the 23d of January. On that day the Earl of Abingdon, immediately after the houfe met, adverted to the circumftance, and gave notice of his intention to move for the Judges to be fummoned, which motion he accordingly made on the 27th; and on the 4th of February again brought the fubject into difcuffion, by moving two refolutions declaratory of the illegality of fuch voluntary fubfcriptions. In every debate which took place on thefe feveral motions, Lord Camden was particularly decided in the fentiments he then gave, and earneftly afferted the unconftitutional and illegal tendency of every meafure by which the crown might obtain, without parliamentary fanction, the difpofal of fums of money raifed without parliamentary authority.

On the 22d of January, being the 3d day of

of meeting after the adjournment, the subject was incidentally touched in conversation in the house of commons; and on the 4th of February the affair of the subscriptions was again introduced in the debate; in both which instances Lord Ashburton, then Mr. Dunning, treated the measure with the utmost severity, and pointedly condemned it as unconstitutional and illegal; and on the 2d of April a specific motion was made by Mr. Wilkes, for leave to bring in a bill to prevent similar practices. In this motion he was most strenuously supported by Mr. Burke. In this case also the crown does not appear to have been the original promoter of the measure, though it certainly conceived itself justified in accepting the *voluntary offerings* of its patriotic subjects, a measure decidely condemned by Lord Camden and Mr. Dunning.

The next and last precedent to be examined, is that of 1782; and, as it seems to be that case on which administration appear to have placed most dependance for defending their present measure, it is most necessary to give it a distinct and particular attention. This may be accomplished with the less difficulty, and to greater advantage, inasmuch as the documents relating to it are all in existence, and no dispute can arise from an inaccurate remembrance of the facts

facts relating to it. It is somewhat singular, that those to whom the task of defence was allotted, should, under a knowledge of the notoriety of these circumstances, have ventured to practice such an unexampled degree of sophistry as that which has been exerted on the present occasion; a sophistry which could have no pretension to success, but that which originated in its own incomprehensible refinement, and which could entertain no hope of escaping detection, but through the *indolent inattention, or too great confidence* of those to whom it was addressed. It is sincerely to be lamented, that the effect which it has produced, should have created the necessity of exposing it to the public.

The first documents to be considered, are the letters of the Secretary of State of that time (Lord Shelburne), and the plan proposed. The first letter is a circular address to the chief magistrates of the several great towns; the second is one to the Lord Lieutenants of the different counties, enclosing that to the Mayors of boroughs or cities; and the third is a distinct letter of a different description, addressed to the Lord Mayor of the city of London. These several letters were all accompanied by an inclosed plan, which is the 4th of the four first documents

which

which I propofe to examine. Upon the face of the two firſt of thefe letters* it appears, that the fole object of adminiſtration in fending them out, was to collect information as to the moſt effectual means by which the energy of the country might at a critical period be called forth. They were not fummonfes to act, but fimply to deliberate upon the beſt mode of acting; and the plan which accompanied them, could only be confidered as fuggeſting hints upon which the letters themfelves called for improvement. The plan was *recommended* to be taken *into immediate confideration*, and a report to be made of whatever *obfervations* might occur for carrying it into *execution*. It was to be confidered as a *propofition* of a temporary plan, which *being adopted* or *improved*, might tend to make a refpectable addition to the national force at home; and the obfervations which might arife were required to be communicated, in order that they might be fubmitted to the confideration of his majeſty; while the plan itfelf can appear in no other light, than as a collection of hints for the approval of the counties, to be fubmitted, firſt, to his Majeſty, and afterwards to Parliament, *before execution*; becaufe it is to be obferved, that the pro-

* App. A and B.

pofal

posal is, that all expences *shall be paid by government, but not by subscription*. The troops so raised, were to be subject to military discipline; and that in case of actual service, and of any personal disability in consequence of such service, the persons so disabled should be entitled to the same advantages with regular soldiers, and the same bounties extended to the widows of such as might fall in the proposed service. These provisions could not by any means have been carried into execution without a previous parliamentary sanction; and that such a sanction would have been required, had the plans proposed been ultimately adopted in toto by the king's ministers, may very fairly be presumed from the circumstance of an act, viz. 22 Geo. III. c.   having passed, to authorize the execution of so much of the plan as it was thought expedient to adopt.

The letter to the Lord Mayor of London[*] which is of a different complexion from those to the counties and boroughs, as it goes beyond the line of enquiry, and calls for a repetition of exertions which had on *former occasions* been successfully employed, is also an additional proof that the minister did not think himself justified in making such an application *generally* through-

[* App. (C.)]

out

out the kingdom; for, knowing that the city of London was permitted to have troops appropriate to itself, he calls upon the chief magistrate to take the most effectual means to prepare those troops for service, in case of any sudden necessity; and at the same time requests an opportunity of *conferring* with the Lord Mayor *as to any additional exertion which the city of London may think proper to adopt.* This letter is evidently a letter of something more than consultation. It is a letter of consultation, where it calls upon the city to *advise* as to the best means of doing that which had not been *usually* done; but it is also a letter of *requisition,* upon points in which the minister saw that *he might constitutionally require*; and it is justifiable to infer from thence, that he made no requisition any where else, because he was conscious that he had *no right* to make any. Knowing that the city was in possession of *legal* means of exertion, he calls upon it to carry those means into execution; but feeling also that the counties were in the lawful possession of *none* but what had been *already* called forth, he addresses *them only* in the way of advice, to consider what *would be* the most eligible mode of encreasing their powers of defence.

It should seem from the conduct of those who have lately supported the minister in his proposal of subscriptions, that they were fully sensible

sible that this was the only conclusion to be drawn from the letters themselves. No other satisfactory reason can be given for that curious artifice of sophistry to which they had recourse, I mean the artifice of collecting the intent of those letters, not from the plain expressions of the letters themselves, which they were evidently conscious would not bear the construction they chose to give them; but from the various answers which were sent from the different quarters whither the letters had been addressed. In order to illustrate in the most forcible manner the ideas which have arisen in my mind on this subject, I will beg leave to put a case, personally, which every man may answer for himself. I will suppose the case of two persons, one of whom simply consults the other as to the best mode of relieving himself from a present state of poverty, and that the person consulted happening to be of a profligate disposition, recommends the murdering and plundering of the first wealthy person he may chance to meet. It appears to me, that after the example of such sophistical reasoning, the unfortunate being to whom such advice might be so accidentally addressed, though he were filled with the utmost abhorrence for such crimes, might, upon an equal foundation of reason and justice, be charged as a robber and an assassin, as the precedent of 1782 be be stigmatized for soliciting subscriptions, because some were proffered, in *answers* to *letters* which contained not one syllable referring to such contributions. But, as if the injustice of conclusions drawn from such a source was not sufficiently glaring, not only the *collection* of answers was *partially produced*, but even the answers which were brought forward were *partially quoted*. You, Gentlemen, who are distinguished ornaments of your profession, are not to be now told for the first time, that evidence, when mutilated in any degree, carries no weight with it in a court of justice; but when that mutilation is evidently the work of the parties themselves, does it ever fail to rouse the indignation of the court, and to stamp with disgrace the man who has attempted the deception? God forbid that the public should meet with less justice than an individual; they are at least entitled to equal attention, and not to *less respect*. But in regard to the question, as it is affected by these answers, it is at present highly favourable to the cause of the people. The letters appear to have been only letters of enquiry; ministers have affirmed that they were letters of solicitation; and this they infer from the tenour of *particular* parts of *selected* answers. But when those who make sturdy assertions, at the same time *refuse to produce* what they call proofs, while they are known to have

have the neceffary evidence, if any fuch evidence really exifts, in their own poffeffion, they afford a complete prefumptive teftimony againft themfelves, in favour of every perfon who contradicts them, upon any appearance of foundation.

It has been afferted on the other hand, by thofe who conducted the meafure of 1782, that in thefe anfwers, fome gave an account of what had been done in former times, fome what had been lately doing, fome what they propofed to do; in fhort, fome giving one advice, fome another. Indeed thofe exracts which have been produced have no tendency to contradict this pofition; on the contrary, they rather ftrengthen it.

Confcious, again it fhould feem, that the inferences drawn from thefe *anfwers* to the letters, were directly contrary to thofe warranted by the letters themfelves; not content with applying partial quotations and refufing complete inveftigation, they expect to bolfter up their argument by an affected concern, that they are unable to confirm their affertions by the evidence of thofe replies which were *probably* written to fuch anfwers; becaufe, fay they, fuch replies are not *now* to be found in the office*. Such an argument, it muft be confeffed, may, with great propriety, be ufed

* App. (D.)

by

by the prefent adminiftration, if we reflect upon the little hefitation with which the Secretary of State for the home department throws upon his office the blame of a *fuppofed inaccuracy*, as unprecedented as it is unaccountable. It would certainly be very extraordinary that no copy of thofe anfwers fhould be to be found in the office, if indeed any fuch anfwers had been written, efpecially when it is clear, that *every other paper* relative to this tranfaction has been preferved with the greateft exactnefs. And if any fuch replies had been written, admitting that the office copy might have been miflaid, it would be ftill more fingular, that not one fhould have been traced and produced from among the various dependents and wide connexions of government, to fome of whom fuch replies muft have been addreffed. So that we may, without any extraordinary exertion of faith, give full credit to the minifter of that period, who declared lately in his place, that *not one anfwer was ever written:* for what ftronger proof can exift, than fuch complete filence, to fhew that this meafure *could* only be confidered by thofe who fet it on foot, to be the beft means of obtaining information. If the object of the minifters had really been fomething more than mere enquiry, is it confiftent with common fenfe to fuppofe, that he would have

contented

contented himſelf with thoſe advantages to be derived from the ſuggeſtions or information communicated to him, when it is evident, from the anſwers in general, that the zeal of the country was prepared for great and well intended exertions? Is it probable, that if ſubſcriptions had been his object, he would have heſitated to accept them with gratitude, when the offer was not only actually made, but when the offer ſo made was alſo *purely voluntary?* Is it likely that he would have neglected ſo fair an opportunity of encouraging the *patriotiſm* of others, by praiſing the readineſs of thoſe who had ſet ſo *laudable* an example? Upon a review of theſe arguments, I do not ſee what further reaſoning is requiſite to produce a clear conviction, not only that this letter of Lord Shelburne was a mere letter of enquiry, but that it was ſo conſidered by thoſe to whom it was addreſſed, and conſequently, in every reſpect utterly inapplicable as a precedent to confirm the propriety of the preſent meaſure. But as truth cannot be tried by too many teſts, let us take another line: let us ſuppoſe for a moment, that inſtead of being a plan *to be* adopted or approved, as the letter ſays, that it was a plan *already* adopted; in which caſe I do not deſpair of being able to ſhew, that theſe two plans of 1782 and 1794 do do not agree in any one point; but, above all, in the principal point which creates the present question, viz. that of subscriptions.

1st. According to the plan of 1782*, the officers were to be appointed from among the gentlemen of the neighbourhood, by commission from the crown, or the lord lieutenant, *but at the recommendation of the chief magistrate* of the town in which the corps should be raised. According to that of 1794, the officers are to receive their commissions from the crown, without any recommendation whatever.

2d. According to the plan of 1782, it was intended that the officers should be possessed of some certain qualification. According to that of 1794, none is to be required.

3d. According to the plan of 1782, the times of exercising the men were to be so selected as not to interrupt their respective labours. According to that of 1794, those periods are to be fixed at the mere will of the crown, by a warrant from the king.

4th. The plan of 1782, *absolutely restrains* the employment of such corps, except in cases of actual invasion or rebellion; that of 1794, permits their being employed on such occasions, without forbidding such employment on any other account.

* App. Ed. (F.)

5th.

5th. The plan of 1782 throws the whole expence upon government; and by propofing no other mode of fupply, creates the neceffity of a *previous application to parliament.* That of 1794, by propofing a fubfcription*, while it charges government with the expence, furnifhes it alfo with a *poffible means of defraying that expence independent of parliament.*

You, Gentlemen, may perhaps argue, that thefe are *cobweb diftinctions,* as a noble Lord was pleafed to call the difference between fubfcribing a mufquet, and fubfcribing a guinea to buy a mufquet; or, as it was ftated to the Houfe of Commons, between fubfcribing money and money's worth. If thofe diftinctions are but as accurate and as powerful as that which conftitutionally exifts between the cafes fuppofed by the noble Secretary of State, and thofe who fupported the meafure in the Lower Houfe, I am confident I fhall never have to blufh for the flimfey texture of my reafonings. The fact is, that this cobweb diftinction conftitutes the true queftion of debate; it brings forward the main point of fubfcription; it involves the caufe of all danger, the means of extra parliamentary fupply; and although the people of England may fee no caufe of apprehenfion in a *guinea fubfcription,* the precedent, if un-

* App. (G.)

condemned,

condemned, may be cited hereafter to sanction the subscription of a million of guineas. It is a doctrine replete with the most fatal consequences. If the people submit, it must produce despotism; if they resist, it is but the harbinger of anarchy. Let those who maintain such positions, look a little to the events which may follow the attempt to establish such doctrines, Whether the prospect presents to their view their own slavery, and that of their fellow citizens, or whether, in the distant resistance of a multitude enraged by repeated oppressions, they survey the probable ruins of a pile, the pretended object of enthusiastic admiration, let them pause a moment, and consider what, in either of these events, will be the reflections of *their* consciences. In such a situation they must feel what they have themselves occasioned; and though the resentment of an offended people should consign them to that destruction they intended for others, still the means of expiation would bear no proportion to the magnitude of the crime. But let us, before we drop this subject of the precedents, examine a little this cobweb distinction, and see whether in reality it will not bear a little more brushing than is necessary to clear away most other cobwebs. The question which has been advanced, and which the upright guardians of our freedom have suffered to pass uncontradicted, is, that there is in substance no difference between a contribution of any given number of musquets, and one of a sum of money to purchase a certain quantity of arms.—Very few words will be sufficient to point out the distinction, which is nothing less than the distinction between that which is legal and constitutional, and that which is illegal and unconstitutional. It ought to be remembered, that it is the *possibility* of evil which constitutes the unconstitutional tendency of every measure; and therefore, until we can demonstrate the possible evil which may arise from any particular proposition, we are not authorized to hold forth that proposition as hostile to our constitution. I will put the case of accepting ships upon the same footing with the acceptance of a stand of arms. The noble Lord who has made this question, will probably tell us, that an acceptance on the part of the crown, of a ship of war, from one of its subjects, can be productive of no possible evil. We will readily grant this assertion to be true, so long as the king can get neither men to man that ship, nor money to pay those men, without the assistance of parliament; but if the subscription is a sum of money, though the subscribers may have given it for a particular purpose, still if the crown is disposed to appropriate it to any other, those who granted the money, in this case, have no means of controul-

ing

ing or preventing such a misapplication. That power of controul and prevention resides only with the Parliament; and it is by possessing the *sole power* of supplying the wants of the crown, that they are enabled to exercise such an authority. Suppose the case of a great armourer offering as a voluntary present to the king, a stand of ten thousand arms. I am not aware of any principle of the constitution which would be violated by the acceptance of those arms, for they are perfectly harmless until they are put into the hands of soldiers; and soldiers can be by *no means* * constitutionally raised without the legislative sanction. The levying a body of men without such sanction, is illegal, because those men may be immediately, *instantaneously* employed to the most dangerous and unconstitutional purpose. Upon the same principle it is that money cannot be raised but by the same authority. It is money which gives the means of exertion; and money acquired independent of Parliament, presents the

---

* Whenever any doubt has arisen respecting the power of the crown to raise, *in time of war*, a greater number of men than what has been voted by Parliament, the arguments in favour of this prerogative have always been drawn from the supposed impossibility of making or paying such levies *without money*, and a concession that *no money* can be obtained without the assistance of Parliament. This, if it were true, would, on the part of the constitution, be nothing less than a mockery, an insulting triumph over the weakness of the crown, by telling the king he may do what he pleases, while it is previously settled that he can, in fact, do nothing.

means of exertion independent of the fame authority. But the mere poffeffion of a fhip, or a ftand of arms, cannot produce any fuch effect; if it could, at the clofe of every war, the fhips inftead of being laid up fhould be all burnt, and the arms inftead of being carefully laid afide fhould be all broken to pieces.

Let us now examine this queftion, as it is referrable to conftitutional principles. The conftitution of this country, in *placing* the purfe in the hands of the commons, has two diftinct objects in view. The firft is, to prevent the fubject from being oppreffed by unneceffary burthens; the next is, to check the executive power in the exercife of its prerogative of declaring war. Whenever the commons pafs a bill of fupply, they at the fame time, except in fome fpecific cafes, determine alfo to what particular purpofes the fums fo granted, fhall be applied. Jealoufy and diftruft are fo pointedly the characterftic features of this principle, that my only aftonifhment is, from whence the doubt can have arifen as to the unconftitutional tendency of the meafure; for I am clear that no means can be invented, by which the crown may attempt to obtain money from the fubject without the previous fanction of parliament, which would not directly militate againft one or both of thefe objects. It is true, that that cannot be confidered as a burthen which is so far given voluntarily that it may be witholden; and therefore granting for the present that these subscriptions are strictly voluntary, that every subscriber is conscious within himself that he is acting under no compulsive influence, the first of these principles which I have mentioned, viz. the prevention of oppression, does not immediately appear to be invaded; since the only definition of oppression with which I am acquainted is, the being compelled to do something, which by choice we should otherwise avoid; or the being prevented from doing that which, were we masters of our own actions, we should wish to do. This concession, which is merely temporary, I have made, because I can conceive cases wherein the gift shall be *perfectly voluntary*. I do not intend by any means to allow, that it is so in this instance; on the contrary, I trust that I shall be able to prove, that the present case is attended by circumstances which partake so much of the nature of compulsion, that it is even within the reach of the first object of our constitution, which retains the purse in the power of the commons, in order to prevent the subject from being oppressed by unnecessary burthens; but I do positively assert, that *no case* can arise in which a voluntary subscription of any kind, and for any of the purposes of government, will not militate

against

against the right of the parliament to controul the executive power, so as to check it in the exercise of its prerogative of declaring war.

It was a saying worthy of the character from whom it came, our first Edward, that "that which concerned all, should be agreed to by all." It is a maxim of the most liberal description, and capable of the most extensive application. That which concerns all, should be agreed to by all; and how can such consent be expressed, but through the constitutional voice of the parliament; or, are there any measures of a public nature which the crown can adopt, or any grants which can be made, which do not immediately concern the community at large? Had this question been put to Lord Coke, he would probably have answered from his own writings; "The commonalty of England cannot grant but by parliament*." Whenever there exists a general disposition in the people to make liberal contributions in favour of any particular measure, what means of expressing that disposition can they use so consistent with their own dignity, or with that of the first executive magistrate, as through the medium of their representatives? Or, at what moment can taxes be imposed with

* 2 Inst. 530.

less odium, or with more efficacy? The system of begging, is a disgrace to the crown from whence it *originates*, and injurious to the public cause, as it tends to promote an impression that the great constitutional source of supply, by parliamentary taxation, is nearly exhausted. But, supposing the fact really to be, that the people in general are well disposed towards such voluntary subscription, the crown can have no ground for knowing that circumstance, but the ground of presumption; because the people cannot collectively express their sentiments except through their representatives; and no individual can in his private capacity, and of his own mere authority, constitutionally perform any act in which the interest of the whole community is in any degree concerned. It is much oftener in our power to prevent injuries, than it is to repair them when committed; and it is the great property of wisdom to foresee difficulties, and by that means to be enabled to prevent misfortune. Upon this principle it is, that one of the chief objects of our constitution, has ever been in the first instance to prevent the executive authority from obtaining money without the consent of Parliament; because, although it claims at the same time the right of controuling the disposition of the money which is granted, yet it is well aware that it has no means of enforcing that claim, but by its power of refusing all future supplies, in case that claim is disallowed: and the real danger to the constitution, or the real injury done to the people, does not depend so much on the temporary privation of a sum of money, as it does upon the manner in which the money is applied: for it is easy to conceive a beneficial appropriation of sums obtained by unconstitutional means; in which case, though the example may be pernicious, yet the effect actually produced in practice, is for that time advantageous. But if the King can legally receive from certain of his subjects voluntary subscriptions, what mode can Parliament effectually adopt to prevent any dangerous disposition of that money, supposing it to be the inclination of the crown to employ the produce of such subscriptions in any manner injurious to the country, and contrary to the expressed sentiments of Parliament? They may remonstrate, but if the crown is obstinate, they cannot enforce that remonstrance; they have parted with the means of prevention; they have given away that inestimable barrier of the constitution, which secures to the people a tranquillity, such as the ambition of a sovereign cannot interrupt without their connivance; they have put arms into the hands of the enemy, and they have no means of resistance left but that of arming themselves.

Supposing this mode of application to be legal,
still

still the proof of the public approbation of the measure it is intended to promote, must depend upon the universality of the subscription; but it does not follow that the *success* aimed at, will also depend upon the same circumstance: for it is easy to suppose a case where the private interest of a combination of wealthy individuals, when in unison with the wishes of the sovereign, shall call forth such strenuous exertions as may enable the crown to effect its own purposes, and to gratify the views of such persons at the expence of the interests of the rest of the community. I conceive that the existence of such a possibility, is sufficient to bring the case within the restrictive influence of our laws. Far be it from me to insinuate, that such is the disposition of our present gracious sovereign; but the history of past times teaches us, that we have had sovereigns of a very different character, and the history of human nature gives us reason to conjecture, that such dispositions may again fill the seat of royalty. Then will it be that the pernicious consequences of this doctrine will be practically felt, and posterity have to curse that servility, which could sacrifice the law of the land to gratify the caprice and ambition of a minister. If the jealous temper of the constitution is ever to be

called

called forth, it cannot be exerted at a more proper moment than when a King, even the beſt, is attempting to obtain money from private individuals without the previous conſent of Parliament, and without firſt communicating to Parliament the object of its deſtination. The conſtitution ſuppoſes, that where the views of the executive magiſtrate are laudable, the Parliament will join in promoting them; but their power would be very nugatory, if they were not armed with a preventive authority. It would be to but little purpoſe to inveſt them with the power of judging of the laudability of plans, if they had not alſo the means of cruſhing the execution, in caſe they conceived them to be injurious; and if we grant for an inſtant, that the King may find means *conſtitutionally* to obtain money under any device whatever, without the concurrence and aſſiſtance of Parliament, in that conceſſion we deprive the Parliament of their preventive power, and grant to the King the *poſſibility* of doing without any Parliament at all.

The great Algernon Sidney, in one of his diſcourſes on Government, ſays, that " one of the
" reaſons of importance to thoſe nations who,
" though they think fit to have Kings, yet de-
" ſire to preſerve their liberty, which obliges
" them to ſet limits to the power, glory, and
riches

"riches of their Kings is, that they can no
"otherwife be kept within the rules of the
"law; becaufe, adds he, fuch is the propen-
"fity of mankind to corruption, that if he
"whofe intereft and will it is to corrupt them,
"be furnifhed with the means, he will never
"fail to do it." Who can doubt the juftice of this obfervation, or who doubts the defire of an Englifhman to preferve his liberty? The means of prefervation eftablifhed by our conftitution, are correctly ftated in the foregoing paffage. The power of the crown is kept within the limits of the law, by its riches being *totally* derived through, and *wholly* dependent on the will of Parliament ; and its means of corruption are completely cut off, fo long as the conftitution uniformly oppofes every attempt at an extra-parliamentary fupply: but the inftant that the limits of the royal revenue are not dependent on the will of Parliament, the inftant that the means of corruption are placed within the grafp of the crown, by its being enabled by *any device* to obtain and to appropriate fums of money without a previous Parliamentary fanction, that inftant the liberty of the people muft expire; or if it is kept alive, its exiftence muft depend on exertions calculated to produce the moft violent confequences. Thefe arguments are all applicable, I conceive, to a cafe yet

more

more strongly favourable to the pretensions of the crown, than that particular case which has given rise to the present discussion; they are, I apprehend, declaratory of the incapacity of the crown, even *to receive* any subscriptions which shall have been strictly and bonâ fide voluntarily offered by the subject. But in the present instance the case is infinitely stronger against the crown, because here the crown has been the *first mover*; the subscriptions have been actually set on foot under the authority of a *motion from the crown*, without any application or intimation, either previous or subsequent, to Parliament for their concurrence.

The distinction which has been made in this case, by some distinguished characters is, doubtless, taken with infinite ingenuity; and certainly the circumstance of the measure having originated in a recommendation from the crown, creates a still greater violation of the principles of the constitution, than if it were simply the case of the crown's receiving a sum of money raised by a *mere voluntary subscription*, where the plan had been proposed by the subscribers themselves, without any intimation whatever from any other quarter. That such receipt and appropriation is greatly exaggerated by any attempt on the part of the crown to promote the measure, I have no doubt; but I cannot for a moment allow, that even the

voluntary

voluntary fubfcription, though infinitely lefs likely to be productive of ferious inconvenience, is not totally incompatible with the fpirit of our conftitution; becaufe it muft be granted, that any means by which the crown is enabled to difpofe of money independent of parliament, in the exercife of its dominion over England, is highly fubverfive of the rights and liberties of the people.

The poffeffion of riches is neceffarily attended by power, and the criterion of defpotifm has ever been regulated by the power of obtaining money. Wherever that power is, there the fupreme authority muft ultimately refide, becaufe the power of raifing money involves in it alfo that of difpofing of the money when raifed; and whether the fum be levied in the form of a tax under the fanction of parliament, or by the perfuafion of the fovereign under the name of a benevolence or fubfcription, the influence to be derived from it muft flow from the difpofal of it. There is in this country but one body, to which the conftitution has entrufted an unlimited power, and that is the fupreme legiflative affembly of the kingdom, compofed of the king, the lords fpiritual and temporal, and the commons, or reprefentatives of the people. They, and they only, when affembled in their legiflative capacity, are

poffeffed

poffeffed of that undefined and abfolute authority, which enables them to exclaim *with effect,*

"Sic volo, fic jubeo, ftet pro ratione voluntas."

The fpecial prerogatives or privileges which have gradually annexed themfelves to thefe feparate orders, each in their refpective capacities, are all reftricted by certain fundamental principles, which cannot be violated without a manifeft injury to the conftitution. By thefe principles it is that thofe prerogatives of the crown which do exift, are fo defined and limited as to be rendered incapable of oppreffion; and in conformity to the fame principles it is, that others which the ambition of princes might induce them to claim, are not fuffered to exift at all. "Prerogative," fays Mr. Locke, "is the difcretionary power of acting for the public good, where the pofitive laws are filent." If then the conftitution was abfolutely filent as to the moft advantageous mode of raifing money, if indeed there was no authority under the fanction of which the appropriation of the money when raifed was to be directed, we fhould in that cafe have fome reafonable ground for prefuming that, becaufe it was requifite for the well being of the ftate, that fums of money fhould be regularly obtained for the purpofes of government; and becaufe no fpecific mode, by which fuch fupplies fhould be raifed,

raifed, was marked out by the law, and no authority eftablifhed, by which the expenditure fhould be regulated, therefore the apparent neceffity of fuch meafures naturally implied the exiftence of a difcretionary power in the crown for this purpofe. But, is the conftitution indeed filent on this head? Is our fyftem of fupply, in fact, fo undefined as to give any colourable pretenfion for the exercife of this prerogative on any fuch ground? or rather let me afk, whether, in the whole frame of our government, there is any one point which has been examined with fo much attention, or decided upon with fo much jealoufy, as that particular article, the difpofal of the public purfe? Do not the commons on all occafions of fupply, claim, and is not their claim invariably allowed, the *fole* arrangement on this fubject? Do they ever fuffer the interference of the lords to have any effect? Is there an amendment which could be made by the lords, which when returned to the commons, would not produce an inftantaneous rejection of the bill? If the commons, then, claim fuch an unlimited privilege in fettling all modes of fupply, as not to fuffer even an amendment by the lords to pafs without rejecting the bill in toto, is it confiftent with common fenfe, to fuppofe that conftitution which grants to them fuch a prerogative, intends to circumvent the whole plan of liberty, by allowing

allowing to *the crown*, not only to devise means of raising a supply, but also to direct the appropriation of it without a parliamentary sanction? To close this division of the question, I am confident that it would be impossible to state any one point in our constitution, in which the law, and the reasons of that law, are so clear, and in which any interference on the part of the crown would be so justly odious, as in that which relates to the *means* of raising money.

The next and last point which arises in this branch of my argument, as referring to the principles of the constitution, unconnected with the actual practice on this subject, and independent of *the law* of the land, is, that it is impossible for the crown constitutionally to *move* the subject to a *voluntary benevolence*; for this reason, that any recommendation from the crown, carries with it an influence nearly approaching to compulsion. And this particular part of the question has its foundation in something, if possible, even stronger and more impressive than any force which reasoning *alone* can apply; it is capable of a solution by an appeal to every man's own heart. Let every one consult his own feelings, and then declare how he should chuse to resist in his own proper person, any request which might be made by the crown, however inconvenient the compliance might be to his previous arrangements,

or

or however inconsistent with his ideas of that conduct which ought to be observed by the executive magistrate, as prescribed by the constitution; and whether, in fact, he should not consider such a request to him, in the same light in which Sir John Eliot appears to have viewed the loans of Charles the First, when in his petition from the Gate-house, where he had been confined for not acceding to the requisition of a loan, he stiles all such requests to the subject, *tacit* and *implied commands?*

It is true that, in the present instance, there are no legal means by which any person can be *compelled* to subscribe; but are there indeed no other modes of compulsion by which any particular effect may be produced, save those which the law has provided? are there not means which are *contrary* to law? and are there not also means which possess different shades of criminality (for nothing can be illegal without being in some degree criminal) by involving different degrees of compulsion? If there is any one circumstance attending this requisition, calculated to counteract the inclination of a man's mind as it is directed by his reason, such circumstance, whatever it may be, amounts in its effect to a compulsion, and furnishes an additional ground for determining that the measure is directly invasive of the principles of the constitution. Let us trace this question

question by examples. I will suppose a body of private individuals *spontaneously* to assemble together, and to agree among themselves to promote a subscription, to be disposed of under their immediate inspection, for the augmentation of bounties for the purpose of facilitating the levy of a body of troops which has been ordered to be raised by *authority of parliament*. Such an undertaking would, I conceive, be strictly constitutional and legal, because it originates with those, whose opinions or wishes cannot be supposed to carry with them an influence capable of inducing any other person to forego his own inclination, that is, to act under any degree of compulsion, not warranted by law; and because the object to be promoted, has previously received the approbation of parliament. Besides, in a case of this sort, the possibility of misapplication to any dangerous extent, is so very remote, and the means of punishment and redress are so instantaneous, that it is unnecessary for the constitution to exercise its preventive power, and to forego the probability of a certain advantage. I will suppose another case, where a subscription shall be set on foot by a society of private individuals, for the purpose of raising and paying a body of troops, without the previous sanction of Parliament. Such a measure would certainly be highly unconstitutional and illegal, even though the object of it should be in itself innocent.

cent. The violation of constitutional principle in such a measure would not depend on the fact of compulsion; the measure itself would, under such circumstances, be nothing less than an assumption, without the assent of Parliament, on the part of private persons in their self-created capacity, of the exercise of one of the duties of the executive magistrate, in the exercise of which duty that magistrate must himself depend on the will of Parliament for the means of its execution. Now what is the case in the present instance? The crown unites itself to a body of individuals for the purpose of promoting subscriptions without the previous sanction of Parliament; the produce of which subscriptions may afterwards be applied, equally independent of the will of Parliament, to the raising and paying of troops. Here then is an instance yet more unconstitutional than the last. Let us see in what its *greater* unconstitutional tendency consists. It cannot be because it is calculated to give to the crown the disposal of a purse uncontrouled by the legislature; because that simple effect might be equally produced from the last example; since the purse might as easily be laid at the king's feet, as its contents expended in the collection and payment of an armed force. The truth is, that the additional violation in this instance, depends on the addition of the royal influence, which, to every

person

person at all acquainted with the difpofition of the human mind, muft be acknowledged at all times to carry great weight with it, but to be particularly calculated to produce an effect very different from, or at leaft infinitely more extenfive than that which would arife from the inclination being left to flow in its own natural channel; at a time too, when the imaginations of mankind are heated by every kind of artifice, and when thofe who can look on with an impartial and difinterefted eye, cannot breathe even a figh of oppofition to any one meafure of government, without incurring the odious ftigma of *factious republicans*.

The relative duties between a king and his people are, command and obedience: and the fovereign ceafes to be a king when his fubjects ceafe to obey. In defpotic governments, the command iffues directly from the fovereign; in a free ftate it is controuled, not by the people, but by an umpire chofen between the parties; and this umpire is felected, not becaufe the people, if they think fit to exert it, have not the power to prevent oppreffion, but becaufe that power is likely to be exercifed with more difcretion by a body which, being raifed above the reft of the people by the importance of its functions, and by being confcious of its own confequence, is thereby removed to a greater diftance from the influence

influence of thofe turbulent paffions, and oftentimes unreafonable prejudices, which fway the conduct of every multitude, and at the fame time, by being brought nearer to the level of the prince, is placed further beyond the probability of being dazzled by the luftre of royalty, and is by that means rendered *lefs likely* to be perfuaded into the adoption of meafures hoftile to the true interefts and liberty of the people. Whenever the crown fhall think fit to difclaim, *in any degree*, the fuperintendence of Parliament, the intervention of the conftitutional medium of intercourfe between itfelf and its fubjects, it muft not be furprifed if the people fhould follow the example, and take the management of their own affairs into their own hands.

Such I take to be the intent of our conftitution. The queftion then fimply is, whether the crown, by any application to the people, otherwife than through the medium of Parliament, is not guilty of exercifing an influence as inconfiftent with our maxims of government as any other attempt would be whofe object was to exercife an *independent* authority. The queftion here is not, whether a man can refift the demand—phyfically he certainly can; but the point is, whether a man, who, in his heart, difapproves of the meafure, may not be influenced by fome confufed notions of apprehenfion, which fhall induce

duce him to act in contradiction to his inclination? This is a question which every man must decide from his own feelings. Upon thefe feveral grounds, and from a perfuafion that fuch notions do exift, it is, that my mind has adopted a complete conviction, that it is impoffible for the crown to take any fteps without the previous fanction of Parliament, towards exciting a voluntary contribution, by private individuals, without incurring, in fome degree, the guilt of violating the fundamental principles of the Englifh conftitution.

We now come to confider the merits of this queftion as they depend upon the conftruction of the ftatute law of the land.

Whether the right of taxation can exift in the crown, independent of Parliament, is a point which has now been long and happily fettled. The various unfuccefsful ftruggles on the part of the executive power, to obtain this high badge of authority, are every where extant in our hiftories; and the final triumph of the people on every occafion is teftified by folemn ratifications of their unalienable rights by fucceffive parliaments. But though the poffeffion of this power was prevented, yet the crown ever retained an inclination to exercife it: and as we eafily trace from the variety of acts relating to the fubject, the many devices to which the clergy reforted, in order to elude the provisions of the statutes of mortmain; so in regard to this subject, our annals are replete with various instances in which the ingenuity of ministers was exercised with a view to obtain money, without the necessity of resorting to Parliament. One among the many inventions on this subject, to which the subtlety of statesmen gave birth, was, that of benevolences; or, as they were supposed to be, voluntary contributions of the people towards assisting the measures of the government. It is the history of the progress, and the issue of this invention, which we have now to trace through the legal records of this kingdom: and it is no small matter of encouragement to me, to find, that in pursuing this subject, I shall have very little occasion to deviate from that track in which the traveller is directed by those great constitutional landmarks, the rolls and records of Parliament.

In the earlier periods of English history, when the royal revenue was chiefly supplied from the profits of feudal services, we find continual struggles between the king and his people; the one to preserve and encrease those exactions, to which according to the purity of that system the lord was entitled, the other to destroy, or to diminish what was always oppressive, but which, when exercised with any degree of rigour, became intolerable. But at the same time, as these exactions,

tions, however severe, were *in general* due of right, when the people prevailed in obtaining some remission of such hardships, the indulgence is certainly to be considered as proceeding from the sovereign, whose *lawful* prerogative it undoubtedly then was, to *exact* the payment of all such aids as were incident to the feudal system. The feudal regulations being all calculated to keep society together after the manner of one great family, and having the means of defence principally in view, have ever been characterized by a military tendency; and having been engrafted in this country upon a spirit among the people already prone to liberty and warfare, they have, perhaps, greatly contributed towards encreasing that spirit, which has ultimately triumphed over the system which cherished it. But as the origin of feuds was in its nature military, so its provisions never appear to have had in view the possible existence of commerce. Accordingly, as this great source of public opulence, and consequently of *public revenue*, encreased, there grew up with it a contest between the crown and the nation, as to the mode of apportioning what was to be raised from this new branch of wealth, for the public service; the king insisting upon his right of exaction, where no previous regulation had settled the subject, and the people claiming their privilege of consent, by the voice of their

repre-

reprefentatives. This point of exaction was early given up by the crown; and Sir E. Coke in speaking of the statute *de tallagio non concedendo**, says, that it was but the explanation of that branch of Magna Charta relating to merchants, which itself binds the king to *exact no duties but such as are due of old custom.* Still however, another question arose, whether, although the king could not exact but by authority of Parliament, he might not *accept* of such additional duties as the merchants themselves should voluntarily consent to pay. Out of this disputed point, I apprehend, the whole system of benevolence has arisen. We will now trace it through a long series of parliamentary proceedings, beginning with the 25 of Ed. I. † The three last chapters of this statute contain, first, a recital that the people were apprehensive that divers aids and tasks, which they had given of *their own grant and good will, (howsoever they were made)* might turn to a bondage; because such taking by the officers of the crown, might hereafter be found upon the rolls. 2ndly, An enacting clause, that no such aids, tasks, or prises, shall be drawn into custom on any account, or on any pretence whatever. 3dly, That for *no business*, shall such manner of aids, tasks, or prises *be taken, but by the*

---

* 2 Inft. 59.   † App. (H.)

common

common assent of the realm; with a saving clause of such aids as were due by reason of tenure. 4thly, The recital of a particular grievance, viz. a toll of 40 s. for every sack of wool, which the statute calls a maletout, and which, according to Sir E. Coke, is an excessive, and in some statutes means an unjust exaction. And 5thly, an enacting clause, that no such toll shall again be taken without the common assent and good will of the people, together with a saving clause of such customs as *had been before granted by the commonalty aforesaid*.

It appears by Sir E. Coke's exposition of this statute*, that the apprehensions of the people originated in an idea, that the aids which they had granted for the defence of the country, or for some other internal purpose, might possibly be drawn into an example, and exacted for the support of the king in his wars out of the realm, for which they at that time held themselves by no means bound. To remove such apprehensions, parliament annihilates the possibility of applying the past, by enacting, that such aids shall not be drawn into future examples; but in order to secure the effects of this provision, it goes one step further, and enacts, that for *no business* shall such aids be taken, but by consent of

---

* 2 Inst. 528.

Parliament; by that means securing to itself the power of approving or condemning *every* measure before it can be undertaken by the crown. How then can the doctrine of voluntary subscriptions, which has a tendency to make the king independent of Parliament, be supported consistent with the object of this statute, which is to bring the crown as much as possible under the controul of Parliament, by giving to the Commons not only the guardianship of the purse, but also a right of previously deliberating upon the purposes for which the supply is intended? I confess, it seems to me, that the provisions of this act, and the doctrines lately maintained, are so incompatible, that the one cannot stand but by the other's fall.

The next object of this Parliament was to remove an existing grievance, viz. a toll of 40 s. on every sack of wool, which Sir E. Coke tells us, had been imposed *without the assent of Parliament*, and which he defines to be an evil toll or charge. We are not told how this charge was imposed, whether by an absolute effort of royal authority, or by any other means, bearing an appearance of free-will; all we know is, that the imposition, however it was made, was for that time resigned by the crown, though it was some years afterwards resumed and defended, as we shall find, though finally *without success*, upon

the

the ground of having been *freely* granted by the merchants.

The next statute which I shall cite as tending to confirm the ideas I have ventured to offer upon this subject, is that commonly known by the name of the *Statutum de tallagio non concedendo,* passed in the 34 Ed. I.* This statute appears to have been made in consequence of an attempted breach of the 25th of this king, and to be a confirmation of the incapacity created by that act in the crown to take any grants but by authority of Parliament. The words of this statute are, that *nullum tallagium,* &c. *ponatur seu levetur,* the words being, as Sir E. Coke observes in the disjunctive, so " as if it be set by the king, " although it be not levied by him, but by a " subject, as it was in the cases aforesaid, it is " within the purview of this statute †." I submit to the judgment of my readers, whether this disjunctive does not equally warrant the construction, that although the imposition be not set by the crown, yet if it is levied to its use, such an imposition is equally within the purview of this statute; and if this construction be right, the measure of subscriptions, even where it does not originate in a motion from the crown, being nevertheless levied for the crown's use, is contrary to the intent of the 34th of Ed. I. This ſtatute further repeats the prohibition againſt taking the maletout of wool, on any occaſion whatever.

The next which claims attention is the 14 Ed. III. ſtat. 1. c. 21. *

By this ſtatute it appears, that certain aids were due of old cuſtom of certain commodities; that the cuſtom on wool had been particularly limited by Parliament; that the Commons had intreated the King that no more than ſuch uſual or limited cuſtoms ſhould ever be taken, and that this prayer had been granted: and that any further taking than what was ſo ſettled, ſhould be contrary to law, is evident from what immediately follows, where the King prayeth the Parliament, *nevertheleſs,* on account of his great occaſions, that they would grant him for a ſhort time ſome additional ſupply from the articles before-mentioned in the ſtatute. Upon due conſideration of this requeſt, the Parliament conſent to the King's demand, and grant him an additional cuſtom of 40s. on every ſack of wool, and alſo an additional duty on ſome other articles; ſtipulating, at the ſame time, that the grant ſhould only continue in force for a period ſomething ſhort of two years. To theſe terms the King accedes, and in the uſual form of an

* App. (K.)

act

act of Parliament promises, that after the time specified, neither himself nor his heirs shall demand, assess, take, or *suffer to be taken of any Englishman,* more than the old custom established by law. Upon this act Lord Coke observes, that " the King granteth, that after the " time mentioned, he, nor his heirs, would " *take* any more than the old custom*." Upon the words of this statute, and the comment of Lord Coke, we may fairly be entitled to conclude, that it was not only contrary to law *to ask,* but even *to receive* any thing, *otherwise* than with the assent of the other branches of the legislature. Let us see how far this conclusion is supported by the subsequent conduct of Edward, and that of his Parliament. It appears by the rolls of Parliament, that in the 17th year of his reign†, which must have been a *short* time subsequent to the expiration of the period limited for the receipt of the extraordinary aids of 40s. on every sack of wool, &c. Edward *still* continued to receive this additional duty as a *voluntary gift* from the merchants. That the commons complained of this receipt as contrary to the statute, which granted only a duty of half a mark after a stated time, and as contrary to their rights, who must

---

* 2 Inst. 60.   † App. (L.)

be in the end the sufferers by such a voluntary conceffion of the merchants, and therefore prayed that the evil might be immediately remedied. To this requeft the King gave an evafive anfwer, by ftating, that this grant of the merchants could not ultimately charge the Commons, as they had themfelves fettled the faleable price of the feveral commodities, and that it would not be in the power of the merchants to encreafe the charge to their cuftomers. Here for the prefent the matter ended; the Commons content with afferting the illegality; the King fatisfied to evade their demand without abfolutely denying their right. And this complaifance on either fide is not to be wondered at, when we confider the high character and popularity of the King, and the infant ftate of parliamentary power as lodged with the Commons. Upon the fame authority we find the Parliament again complaining, in the 21ft year of this fame King's reign[*], of *his breach of the laws*, by iffuing commiffions under the great feal for obtaining money without their previous grant; and in the 25th[†], the Commons again take up the fubject of the voluntary grant of the merchants. They repeat the grievance arifing from the tax of 40s. and requeft that in future it may neither be *de-*

[*] App. (M.)   [†] (N.)

manded

manded nor *levied*, and that no commissions should be issued in consequence of such single grants, except in *full parliament*; and in consideration of a compliance with this requisition, they offer to legalize this subsidy for half a year, or, perhaps, for a whole year, if the King is really in such great necessity. To this complaint the King pleads in excuse, the continuance of that extreme necessity which first induced him to accept the offer; and this appears to have been so far satisfactory to the Parliament, that they consent to the continuance of this imposition for two years longer. In every one of these instances we find the King seeking some pretence for obtaining money from the subject, without receiving it at the hands of his Parliament, and resorting to such inventions as bear the greatest semblance of *voluntary donations*. Yet, even in all these instances, his Parliament refuses to admit his pleas; and, though the subsidy was generally granted upon the ground of the crown's necessity, yet still the precedent was always opposed, as it might serve for an example to after times. And in the 36th of Edward III. the commons again renew their entreaties [*], that in consideration of their liberality to the King and their readiness to relieve

---

[*] App. (O.)

his

his neceffities, no extraordinary fubfidy fhall be levied after the time limited by them, only the ufual import of half a mark; and that *in future* no impofition on wool can be *granted* by the merchants, or any others, without the affent of the Parliament. The anfwer to this petition of the commons is, " the King wills it."

This tranfaction feems for a time to have ftifled all further attempts at voluntary *donations*. But the triumph of Parliament appears to have only given birth to another device; for the King, finding it in vain to contend for the prerogative of *accepting gifts*, had recourfe to the artifice of *borrowing* of fuch of his fubjects, as fhould chufe to lend him any fums his occafions might require. It fhould feem that fo long as the King confined himfelf to accepting *voluntary* loans, the jealoufy of Parliament was not excited. Probably, as they had originally grounded their objections to the *voluntary grants* of the merchants upon this principle, that fuch donations would ultimately fall upon the people from the additional charges which would be made in the fale of the commodities, fo the fame reafon for apprehenfion did not immediately occur where the means of repayment were previoufly fixed. Thofe nicer diftinctions which have fince added further limitations to regal prerogative, and which have ferved to augment the jealous dif-

position of the constitution in regard to regal encroachments, were then probably unknown; their birth was coeval with the encrease of our wealth, their growth has been proportionate to our progressive importance in the scale of nations. But when any acquiescence in such voluntary loans induced the King to advance one step further, and to attempt at substantiating this device into a matter of right, instead of being what it was at first, entirely matter of favour; when he proceeded to exercise compulsory means in order to obtain loans from those who, upon the first requisition, endeavoured to excuse themselves; we find the commons instantly espousing the cause of the oppressed, declaring all such attempts *to be a scandal to the King, and against the law of the land,* and praying, that in future all persons reasonably excusing themselves, might remain unmolested. This circumstance occurred early in the reign of Richard II. and is proved upon the testimony of the rolls of the Parliament of the 2d of that King*.

I cannot pass this period without noticing the fallacy of an assertion made by Hume, in his 5th volume, where he mentions the encroachments of Elizabeth upon the claims of

* App. (P.)

Parliament.

Parliament to the exclusive privilege of granting money. He affirms in a note, that " in the "second of Richard II. it was enacted, that in "loans, which the King shall require of his "subjects upon letters of privy seal, such as "have *reasonable* excuse of not lending, may "there be received without further summons, "travel, or grief. See Cotton's Abridg. p. 170. "By this law the King's prerogative of ex- "acting loans was ratified; and what ought to "be deemed a *reasonable* excuse, was still left in "his own breast to determine*." The historian lays great stress on the word *reasonable*, as implying a power in the crown to judge of the reasonableness, and accordingly to accept or reject the excuse. This mistake may easily be accounted for, without impeaching the author's intentions. At the time when Hume wrote, the records were not in print; and he appears to have trusted to Cotton, who rejects in his abridgment the preamble of the petition, upon which the whole must depend. For, although the Commons in the enacting part request the crown upon such occasions to admit all reasonable excuses, yet, in the preamble, they have previously *declared*, that all such attempts at exaction are to the *great*

* Vide Hume, 460.

damage

damage and fear of the poor Commons, to the scandal of the King, and against the law of the land. I cannot conceive, that had Mr. Hume seen this record as it is now printed, he would ever have cited it as a ratification of the prerogative of *exacting* loans, since it goes the length of affirming, that all such exactions are contrary to law; and, though it may afterwards desire the crown to admit all reasonable excuses, I should suppose the crown would feel some difficulty in considering *any* excuse as unreasonable in the teeth of such a declaration; and, after all, though the crown should deem the excuse unreasonable, still it cannot *enforce* the demand, *without scandalizing itself, and violating the law.*

After this period, the attempts to raise money by such means appear to have ceased, and not to have been renewed until the reign of Edward IV*: at least our history is either silent on the subject, or I have not been able to discover any transaction of this nature until the second year of this prince; when, according to Stowe's Chronicle†, he issued letters under the privy seal for the purpose of asking a contribution of this description, in order

---

* Vide Parliamentary History. † Stowe's Chronicle and History of Croyland.

to enable him to raife forces againft Henry VI. and which, this author adds, was liberally granted. In or about the 17th year of this King, the hiftory of Croyland mentions, what is there ftiled a new and unheard of impofition, called a benevolence, *whereby every one might give what they would, or rather what they would not;* and the fame authority adds its teftimony to the liberality which was manifefted in the large amount of thefe fubfcriptions. Certainly the author of this account was miftaken in his idea, as to the novelty of this device. The name might be perhaps then, for the firft time, applied; but clearly the invention was of a much earlier origin. This appears from the records of Edward III. already cited: and thofe contributions which were levied on the 2d of Edward IV. could not have been fanctioned by Parliament; becaufe, if the filence of the rolls may be permitted to prove any thing, it proves that no Parliament was holden in that year. But, whatever might be the liberality of the people in their contributions upon thefe particular occafions towards relieving the neceffities of Edward IV. the fpirit of fubfcription feems foon to have fubfided, and the exaction itfelf to have grown into a fubject of complaint. For a very few years fubfequent to this period, the device of benevolence volences having been carried to an intolerable extent, Richard III. in the firſt year, and almoſt one of the firſt acts of his reign, found himſelf under the neceſſity of conſenting to an act of Parliament*, expreſſive of the various evils to which the people had been expoſed, declaring the illegality of all ſuch inventions, particularly ſpecifying the invention of benevolences, and enacting, that in future no *ſuch charges* as have before been taken, ſhall be taken again, but that they ſhall be damned and adnulled for ever.

In the courſe of theſe proceedings, no reference ſeems to have been made to what paſſed in former reigns. The ſyſtem appears to have been taken up as if nothing of the ſort had ever occurred before; and the ſubject of complaint to which a remedy was to have been applied, ſeems on this occaſion to have been wholly confined to the circumſtance of exaction; from whence an inference may certainly be drawn that, *at that time,* a mere voluntary donation was not conſidered as a grievance; and this inference is perhaps ſomewhat ſtrengthened by the next ſtatute which, according to its order of ſucceſſion, I have to cite †. This ſtatute ſets forth, that divers of his Majeſty's ſubjects had ſeverally granted divers ſums of money of their free-wills and benevolence; it then recites, that ſeveral of theſe ſums ·ſo granted had

---

* App. (Q.) † 11 H. 7. c. 10. App. (R.)

not been paid in; and afterwards proceeds to give to the crown, the means of enforcing the payment of such promised grants; and provides, that in case any of the persons having made such promise, shall die before payment made, that in such case the charge shall descend upon the executor of such person, but not upon his heir. Yet allowing to this inference, in its fullest extent, all the force which it can collect, while unconnected with any preceding circumstance, still I do not see upon what principle it can be suffered to stand, when referred back to the transactions of the reign of Ed. III. which even now remain uncontradicted and unrepealed. Until those transactions shall have been condemned by the repeal of what was then agreed to, the statute of Richard III. must be considered as declaring the illegality of *all exactions*, without affecting, in any degree, the question of voluntary benevolences, as it then stood upon the Parliamentary records of the reign of Ed. III. and the statute of H. VII. can only be held to legalize and enforce *for that time*, what would otherwise have been illegal and incapable of taking effect.

I shall pass by the transactions of the reigns of Henry VIII. Mary, and Elizabeth, as being periods of *undisguised* tyranny which will hardly at this time be drawn forth as fit examples for the ministers of the present day. The tyranny of

Henry VIII. being principally supplied from the spoils of the church, his oppressions were not of a nature to be severely felt by the people; and the commons had not then reached that stability of privilege, which has since enabled them to act as much in *preventing* possible evils, as in redressing positive injuries. Mary, fortunately for herself, died before the extravagance of her persecutions had roused the spirits of her people to actual resistance; and the tyrannies of Elizabeth, for tyrannical her reign undoubtedly was, being directed by able statesmen, and generally calculated for the advantage of her subjects, were not likely, while in such hands, to create much opposition; but when these same principles came to be put into practice by her successor, who united to the prejudices of a foreigner, educated with notions still more arbitrary than those of Elizabeth, the disadvantages of a feeble understanding, no other consequences were to be expected than those which followed the errors of James the First. That prince, unequal to comprehend the vast designs of his predecessor's government, saw no difference, or at least thought that there ought to be none, between the expenditure of money for public benefit, and the waste of it for the supply of private extravagance. He was not aware of the encreased opulence, the extended consequence, and the maturer judgment of the

English

English people. That which Elizabeth had rendered palatable by her prudence, he thought might be made subservient to his caprice; and while he struggled for the possession of arbitrary power, his weak understanding could not distinguish those insuperable barriers which must finally stop the career of despotism. It is a melancholy reflection to consider, that Charles the First, with a clearer head and a better heart, fell the victim of his father's principles, which had been so rivetted in him by habit and education, as to give them all the force of prejudices, founded on the best motives, and directed to the purest purposes. Among the chief grievances which excited commotions in the reign of James, the loans and benevolences were the principal; yet even through every transaction relative to these subjects, the utmost precaution, compatible with the exercise of any force at all, seems to have been observed in order to preserve as much as possible the semblance of free-will. Those who refused to contribute to the king's necessities were not at first *ostensibly* punished for such refusal, but were chastized by the silent punishment of being pressed into the king's service in the wars; and Mr. O. St. John does not appear, according to Lord Bacon's statement of his crime, to have been accused for not lending money himself, but for having slandered the King for attempting to raise money in such manner without the consent of his Parliament. It is also to be observed, that Lord Bacon, who was then attorney general, rests the principal part of his defence of the measure itself* which gave rise to Mr. St. John's animadversions, upon the circumstance of those benevolences being *purely voluntary*, as having, among other points of extenuation, or rather exculpation, been given in the first instance without *any motion* from the crown; from whence (if I may be allowed the same privilege of inference so copiously exercised by the champions of this prerogative) I should infer, that he meant tacitly to acknowledge, that had such circumstances existed, the measure would have been illegal. For when a man argues that any particular case is no violation of the law, *because it is unattended by some particular circumstance*, it seems naturally to induce a supposition, that the *concurrence* of such a circumstance would be sufficient to constitute the illegagility of the measure; and those who read the transactions relative to this subject, during the reign of the unhappy Charles, will find a disposition in the arguments which were employed in defence of those who opposed the systems of that period, similar to that which characterizes those of the present. The measure of exaction,

---

* Vide Trial of Oliver St. John, State Trials, Vol. II.

however,

however, was certainly carried to a much greater extent than has hitherto been attempted. We have not yet had imprifonments; we have not yet had the refractory part of the country compelled to go to the wars; but we have had that done which even Lord Bacon, when pleading for the crown, did not attempt to fupport—we have had the crown *moving* the fubject to contributions; exerting that influence which is attached to its high fituation, in order to induce the fubject to part with that money, which cannot conftitutionally be appropriated to public purpofes, but by the direction of Parliament. Let us reflect, that from fmall beginnings, the moft important confequences oftentimes follow. Let us call to mind the trifling beginning, and the fatal end of the meafures of that period, to which we are now arrived. Let us in the prefent inftance, from paft mifconduct, draw leffons of wifdom for future occafions; and by checking every effort towards an unconftitutional extenfion of prerogative, prevent thofe misfortunes which no man can at this moment forefee, and which, when forefeen, no man may be able to prevent. Let us call to minds the notable faying of Lord Coke*, " That when any ancient law or cuftom of Parliament is broken, and the crown poffeffed of

---

* 2 Inft. 528.

" a pro-

"a precedent, how difficult a thing it is to
"restore the subject again to his former freedom
"and safety." But above all, it behoves the
ministers of the crown to consider well the consequences, before they advise the adoption of illegal measures, and thereby lay the seeds of a certain resistance:—they should recollect, that the unfortunate Charles, by provoking a resistance to usurped powers, led the way to the final invasion of his just claims.

The petition of right in the third of this prince, endeavoured to mark out the line of the king's duty, by stating a variety of oppressions which had been practised on the people by the crown, and claiming an exemption from all similar hardships in future. Charles the First, in compliance with the requests contained in this remonstrance, concurred in declaring all the grievances therein complained of, to be contrary to law, and in enacting that none such in future should be practised. Had this ill-fated monarch resolved to abide by the rule which he had himself consented to establish; had he been contented to be guided by the spirit of the act, instead of seeking for the means of evasion from the narrow limits of literal expression; would he but have recollected that he was a limited, not an absolute sovereign; that the kings of England hold their crown, in some degree, at the will, and entirely for the advantage of the people, not by a divine right, originally and immediately proceeding from God, and not with a view to furnish them with a power to be exerted for their sole pleasure, or for their particular ambition; had he but considered that this limitation was created by his *total* dependance on Parliament *for supply*, and that he could never expect to contend for any prerogative of obtaining money, except through that channel, without at the same time preparing himself for the most serious and dangerous consequences; it is probable, that if such had been the tendency of his sentiments, the more melancholy events of his reign would not have occurred. When he had consented, " that thereafter no man should " be *compelled* to make or yield any gift, loan, " or benevolence, without common consent, by " act of parliament," the triumph of the legislature over every attempt at the exercise of such prerogatives was intended to have been decisive. And in fact, so it ought to have been held to be: for the scope of the petition of right, was to declare *every means of extra-parliamentary supply* which had been adopted in preceding times, to be illegal; and among those means must be ranked the subscriptions, for slandering which Mr. Oliver St. John was so severely punished in the reign of James the First; subscriptions which, according to Sir Francis Bacon when pleading in

behalf

behalf of the crown for that profecution*, were of the leaft exceptionable nature, being purely voluntary, *ex mero motu donantis, no not so much as recommended* in the firſt inſtance by the crown. But the prejudices in which Charles had been educated, and the opinions which he had imbibed as to the fanctity of regal authority, could never admit fuch a liberality of conſtruction: on the contrary, they urged him forward, until at laſt he not only aimed at the extenſion of prerogative, by evading the ſpirit, but actually attempted to eſtabliſh an *abſolute* authority, by violating the letter of the law. " Fortunately however, when
" the country emerged from the anarchy and
" miſery of the ſcene which followed, the ex-
" travagance of joy did not extinguiſh a due
" remembrance of the conſtitution. One of the
" firſt acts after the Reſtoration, was a grant of
" tonnage and poundage, with words which
" renewed a part of the former declarations
" againſt taking by prerogative; for it anxiouſly
" recited, that *no rates can be impoſed on mer-*
" *chandize imported or exported by ſubjects or*
" *aliens, but by common conſent in Parliament* †."

The commons however, not fatisfied with the

* Vide Sir F. Bacon's Speech, State Trials, Vol. II.

† Vide Mr. Hargrave's Introductory Note to the cafe of Impoſitions, or Bates's Cafe, in Vol. XI. of the State Trials.

extent

extent of this provision, which might be capable of a construction similar to that which had been put upon former statutes of the same description, and which might be hereafter pleaded as condemning only all *compulsory* efforts of prerogative taxation, seems to have been resolved to exclude all future possibility of raising money, without their previous consent, by an act for that particular purpose; which, by general words, might include every invention by which such an object as the acquisition of money, uncontrouled by Parliament, might be effected. Accordingly, in the next year, being the 13 C. 2.* a statute is passed, containing words declaratory that subscriptions or " benevolences to the crown,
" though voluntary, cannot regularly be made
" out of Parliament." " This statute authorizes
" the king to issue commissions under the great
" seal, for *receiving voluntary subscriptions* for
" the supply of his occasions; but limits com-
" moners to 200*l*. and peers to 400*l*. a piece
" and also the time for subscribing; and con-
" cludes with declaring, that *no commissions or*
" *aids of this nature can be issued out or levied but*
" *by authority of Parliament* †." I deem myself

* App. (S.)
† Vide Mr. Hargrave's Introductory Note to the Trial of Mr. Oliver St. John.

singularly happy in having been able to convey my own impressions on this statute in the words of Mr. Hargrave; because the sanction of such an authority will remove from my conduct the imputation of arrogance in contending with the present attorney and solicitor general, and because his eminent character with the public, as an upright and deeply-learned lawyer, will add the weight of his reputation to those opinions, which, as coming from one not only undistinguished but unknown, would perhaps be thrown aside unread, at all events unregarded. With respect to this construction of this statute, I shall have occasion to add but a very few words. The object, as has been already observed, was to enable the crown to issue commissions under the great seal, for the purpose of receiving certain aids arising from voluntary subscriptions, and at the same time to destroy the possibility of levying such aids in future. In order to oppose the application of this statute to the present question, it has been asserted, that its object was only to prevent the receipt of such aids, through the means of a commission under the great seal. Unfortunately for this assertion, in the prohibition of the future practice of these means of supply, we find that same disjunctive *or* intervening, which was adverted to by Lord Coke in explaining the 34th of Edward I. the words of

the

the 13th Charles II. being, "that no com-
"miffions *or* aides of this nature, can be if-
"fued out *or* levied, but by authority of Par-
"liament;" that is, that no fuch commiffions
can be iffued, *or* aides levied but by fuch authority: that is, according to Lord Coke's reafoning upon, and, indeed, according to the natural
inference to be drawn from this disjunctive, even
though no fuch commiffions fhould be iffued,
ftill abfolutely no fuch aids, viz. *voluntary fubfcriptions*, can be levied. By means of this disjunctive, the commiffions and the aids are made
too diftinct fubjects, entirely independent of each
other; and the provifions of the ftatute for preventing either from being drawn into examples
for the future, muft be applied to each, without
any reference of one to the other. Had the con-
junctive *and* been ufed inftead of the disjunctive
or, then the conftruction might poffibly have
been applied in favour of the prefent meafures,
at leaft the application might have been fupported by fome fhew of reafon; but in confequence of this disjunctive expreffion, the object of which is to diftinguifh and feparate,
fuch an explanation of the meaning of the act
is rendered impoffible. Upon this ftatute the
learned annotator in the ftate trials obferves,
that it was "the aim of the act to condemn
"benevolences by the folicitation of commif-
"fions

"sions from the crown, and to supply the
"defect of the statute of Richard III. and the
"petition of right, both of which point at com-
"pulsive benevolences. The inducement to
"such a declaration of the law probably was
"an idea, that a formal solicitation from the
"crown, must necessarily operate on the minds
"of those to whom it was addressed, with an
"influence almost equal to compulsion. Thus
"at length it seems to be settled by the legisla-
"ture, not only that compulsive benevolences
"are unlawful, but that all commissions from the
"crown to solicit and receive voluntary gifts, are
"also unconstitutional*."

To conclude. I am fully sensible that in the doctrine which I have attempted to establish, I have given a more extensive construction to the statute 13th of Charles II. than has been given to it by Mr. Hargrave. I do not pretend to say that I am right; but even if I am, he is not wrong. The only difference between us I believe to be, that I have been more bold, he more cautious. Upon such subjects I may be permitted to hazard opinions, because I can have only reason and truth for my supporters; in him caution is an absolute duty, as he has also a reputation which might mislead the world; and an

---

* The introductory Note to St. John's Case.

assertion

assertion from him might pass without examination, and be considered as law without enquiry. At all events, however, upon the strength of those arguments which I have myself advanced, together with the sanction of his authority, I may be permitted to consider the point on which I started as decided, namely, that the measures which have been pursued by the present administration for the purpose of raising subscriptions set on foot in consequence of an *original motion* from the crown, are unconstitutional, illegal, and unsupported by any precedent whatever; that consequently they are " grievances found out " and proved*;" which, upon the authority of Sir E. Coke, according to what he calls an excellent precedent, " should be put down and " overthrown by authority of Parliament."

* 2 Inst. (530.)

I am,

Gentlemen, &c.

Lincoln's Inn.

APPENDIX.

(A.)

CIRCULAR.

Whitehall, *May* 7, 1782.

SIR,

HIS Majesty has commanded me to express his firm reliance upon the spirit and loyalty of his People, and his Royal confidence, that during this season of difficulty, their utmost endeavours will not be wanting to give unquestionable proofs of their attachment and emulation for his service. And foreseeing, that by wise, strenuous, and timely preparations, he may not only disappoint or defeat any hostile attempts, but, by appearing strong and united at home, he may be enabled to make the more powerful efforts for maintaining his honour and the public interests abroad, and thereby lay the surest foundation for a safe, an honourable, and a lasting peace; and as the populousness of the *principal towns* and cities of Great Britain naturally offer the *greatest facility*, as well for forming into corps, as for learning the military exercise, ercife, *without lofs of time, interruption of labour, or any confiderable fatigue,* his Majefty has commanded me to tranfmit to you the inclofed *propofition,* which has been fubmitted to his Majefty, as at leaft a *temporary* plan for augmenting the domeftic force of the nation; which *being adopted* or *improved,* according to the circumftance and fituation of the town of which you are the chief magiftrate, may tend to the immediate formation of a great and refpectable addition to the national force at home, on the moft natural and conftitutional principles.

For this purpofe I have his Majefty's commands, to fignify to you his defire and recommendation, that you fhould take the fame *into immediate confideration;* and, *after having* confidered, report to me whatever *obfervations* may occur to you, for carrying into execution a plan, the purpofe of which is, to give fecurity to your own perfons and property, and to the general defence of the kingdom.

I am, &c.

SHELBURNE.

To the Mayor or Chief Magiftrate, &c.

CIRCULAR.

(B.)

CIRCULAR.

WHITEHALL, *May* 7, 1782.

MY LORD, OR SIR,

I HAVE the honour, in obedience to the King's commands, to tranfmit to you a copy of a circular letter, which is to be addreffed to the cities and principal towns in Great Britain. I am to requeft, that your Lordfhip will take the contents into your ferious confideration, and *report to me your obfervations thereupon*, and particularly whatever may occur to you of importance with refpect to the cities or towns within your county, *that I may immediately fubmit them to his Majefty*.

I am, &c.

SHELBURNE.

(C.)

WHITEHALL, *May* 7, 1782.

MY LORD,

I HAVE the King's command to enclofe to your Lordfhip a copy of a circular letter, which I have written by his Majefty's command to the principal cities and towns of Great Britain, inclofing a propofal which has been fubmitted to his

his Majesty, as at least a temporary plan for augmenting the domestic force of the nation. And as his Majesty is disposed to indulge hopes of a general exertion of all his faithful subjects, he is led to encourage with particular confidence an expectation, that his faithful citizens of London will set a prevailing example of activity and zeal on the present occasion; keeping up that character by which they have been so eminently distinguished at many former periods, when their attention to private convenience has given way to their regard for public expediency, and they have from their own body drawn out the most formidable forces, to guard their sovereign and protect their country.

As the means and resources of the capital are greater than the other cities and towns of the kingdom to make essential efforts, his Majesty entertains no doubt of the readiness of his faithful citizens, to shew a degree of exertion proportioned to the superiority of their interests in the safety and welfare of the state.

I must entreat your Lordship to make the proper communication of this proposal; and I shall embrace with great satisfaction the earliest opportunity you will afford me, of conferring with you with respect to the more constant and regular duty of those bodies of men whom you

now

now only occasionally exercise, as well as to any additional exertion which the city of London may think proper to adopt.

I am, &c.

SHELBURNE.

Right Hon. the Lord Mayor,
of the City of London.

(D.)

COPY OF A CIRCULAR LETTER TO THE LORDS LIEUTENANTS OF COUNTIES.

WHITEHALL, *March* 14, 1794.

MY LORD, OR SIR,

FINDING, from an official inaccuracy, that copies of the plans which have been prepared with a view to the augmenting the internal force of this kingdom, have not been communicated to you, I have the honour of inclosing copies thereof herewith.

I am, &c.

HENRY DUNDAS.

(E.)

HEADS OF A PLAN

FOR

RAISING CORPS IN THE SEVERAL PRINCIPAL TOWNS IN GREAT BRITAIN, 1782.

1. The principal towns in Great Britain to furnish one or more battalions each, or a certain number of companies each, in proportion to their size and number of inhabitants.
2. The officers to be appointed from among the gentlemen of the neighbourhood, or the inhabitants of the said towns, either by commission from his Majesty, or from the lord lieutenant of the county, upon the recommendation of the chief magistrate of the town in which the corps are raised.
3. They are to be possessed of some certain estate in land or money, in proportion to their rank.
4. An adjutant or town mayor to be appointed by his Majesty.
5. A proper number of serjeants and corporals from the army, to be appointed for the corps in each town in proportion to their numbers.
6. The said serjeants and corporals, as well as the adjutant or town mayor, to be in the Government's pay.

7. The men to exercife frequently, either in battalion, or by companies, on Sundays and on all holidays, and alfo after their work is over in the evening.
8. Arms, accoutrements and ammunition, to be furnifhed at the expence of Government, if required.
9. Proper magazines or ftorehoufes to be chofen or erected in each town, for keeping the faid arms.
10. The arms and accoutrements to be delivered out at times of exercife only, and to be returned into the ftores as foon as the exercife is finifhed.
11. The adjutant or town mayor to be always prefent at exercife, and to fee that the men afterwards march regularly and lodge their arms in the ftorehoufes.
12. Proper penalties to be inflicted on fuch as abfent themfelves from exercife, as alfo for difobedience of orders, infolence to their officers, or other diforderly behaviour.
13. The above corps not to be obliged on any account, or by any authority whatever, to move from their refpective towns, except in time of actual invafion or rebellion.
14. His Majefty fhall then have power to order the faid corps to march to any part of Great Britain, as his fervice may require.

15. They are on such occasions to act either separately, or in conjunction with his Majesty's regular forces, and be under the command of such general officers as his Majesty shall think proper to appoint.
16. Both officers and men to receive full pay as his Majesty's other regiments of foot from the day of their march, and as long as they shall continue on service out of their towns*.
17. They are to be subject to military discipline, in the same manner as his Majesty's regular forces, during the said time of their being so called out, and receiving government's pay.
18. All officers who should be disabled in actual service, to be entitled to half pay; and all non-commissioned officers and private men disabled, to receive the benefit of Chelsea hospital.
19. The widows of officers killed in the service to have a pension for life.

* Time of service to be named.

HEADS

(F.)

HEADS OF THE PLAN OF 1794.

COPY.

WHITEHALL, *March* 14, 1794.

IN order to provide more completely for the security of the country against any attempts which may be made on the part of the enemy, it may be expedient to adopt some or all of the following measures.

1. To augment the militia by volunteer companies, as was practised in the last war; or by an additional number of volunteers, to be added as privates to each company.
2. To form volunteer companies in particular towns, especially in those situated on or near the sea coast, for the purpose of the local defence of the particular places where they may be raised, according to the accompanying plan, or such other as may, on application for that pupose, be approved of as best adapted to the circumstances of any particular town.
3. To raise volunteer troops of fencible cavalry, consisting of not less than fifty, nor more than eighty per troop, who will be to serve only during the war, and within the kingdom.

The officers will have temporary rank only, and will not be entitled to half pay. The arms, accoutrements, and cloathing, will be furnished by Government, but the levy money for the men to be furnished by the persons who undertake to raise such troops; and the horses to be found by them, but to be paid for, at a reasonable price by Government.

A person raising two troops to have the temporary rank of major; four troops that of lieutenant colonel; and six troops that of colonel.

4. To form other bodies of cavalry within particular counties or districts, to consist of the gentlemen and yeomanry, or such persons as they shall bring forward, according to the plans to be approved of by the king, or by the lords lieutenants under the authority from his Majesty; and the officers to receive temporary commissions from his Majesty; and the muster rolls also to be approved by his Majesty, or by the lords lieutenants, at periods to be fixed. No levy money to be given; and the horses to be furnished by the gentry or yeomanry who compose the corps; but the arms and accoutrements to be supplied at the expence of the public. Such corps to be exercised only at such times as shall be fixed by warrant from his Majesty, or by the approbation
of

of the lords lieutenants; to be liable to be embodied or called out of their counties by special directions from his Majesty, in case of actual appearance of invasion; and to be liable to be embodied or called out of their counties by special directions from his Majesty, in case of actual appearance of invasion; and to be liable to be called upon, by order from his Majesty, or by the lord lieutenant or sheriff of the county, to act within the county, or in the adjacent counties, for the suppression of riots and tumults. In either case, while actually in service, they shall receive pay as cavalry, and be liable to the provisions of the mutiny bill.

5. To enroll and appoint places of rendezvous for a sufficient number of persons in different parishes and districts, particularly in places near the sea coast, to serves as pioneers, or to assist the regular force in any manner that may be necessary, on the shortest notice, in cases of emergency.

GENERAL

(G.)

GENERAL SUBSCRIPTION.

COPY.

Whitehall, *March* 14, 1794.

IT is naturally to be suppofed, that gentlemen of weight or property, in different parts of the kingdom, will feparately ftand forward, in order to carry into execution the feveral parts of the plan for the fecurity of the country. But it feems alfo defirable a general fubfcription fhould be opened, to be applied under the direction of a committee, for the purpofe of affifting in carrying into execution all or any of the meafures therein fuggefted, as circumftances fhall appear to require.

(H.)

25 Ed. I. Statute 1. Chapters 5, 6, 7.

CHAP. 5.

Aids, Tafks, and Prifes, granted to the King, fhall not be taken for a Cuftom.

" AND for fo much as divers people of our
" realm are in fear, that the aids and tafks which
" they have given to us before-time towards
" our

" our wars and other bufinefs, of their own
" grant and good-will, (howfoever they were
" made) might turn to a bondage to them
" and their heirs, becaufe they might be at
" another time found in the rolls, and likewife
" for the prifes taken throughout the realm by
" our minifters in our name; We have granted
" for us and our heirs, that we fhall not draw
" fuch aids, tafks, nor prifes into a cuftom, for
" any thing that hath been done heretofore, be
" it by roll or any other precedent that may be
" founden."

CHAP. 6.

The King or his Heirs will take no Aids, or Prifes, but by the Confent of the Realm, and for the common Profit thereof.

" Moreover we have granted for us and our
" heirs, as well to archbifhops, bifhops, abbots,
" priors, and other folk of holy church, as alfo
" to earls, barons, and to all the communalty of
" the land, that for no bufinefs from henceforth
" we fhall take fuch manner of aids, tafks, nor
" prifes, but by the common affent of the realm,
" and for the common profit thereof, faving the
" ancient aids and prifes due, and accuftomed."

CHAP.

CHAP. 7.

A Release of Toll taken by the King for Wool; and a Grant that he will not take the like without common consent and good will.

" And for so much as the more part of the communalty of the realm find themselves sore grieved with the maletolt of wools, that is to wit, a toll of forty shillings for every sack of wooll, and have made petition to us to release the same;" ' We at their requests have clearly released it, and have granted, that we shall not take that or any other without their common assent and good will, saving to us and our heirs the custom of woolls, skins and leather, granted before the communalty aforesaid.'

(I.)

Statutum de tallagio non concedendo.
Factum anno 34 Ed. 1. stat. 4.

CHAPTER I.

The King or his Heirs shall have no Tallage or Aid without consent of Parliament.

NO tallage or aid shall be taken *or* levied (ponatur *seu* levetur) by us or our heirs in our realm, without the good will and assent of archbishops,

bishops,

bishops, earls, barons, knights, burgesses, and other freemen of the land.

CHAPTER 3.

Nothing shall be taken of sacks of wool by colour of maletolt.

Nothing from henceforth shall be taken of sacks of wool by colour or occasion of maletolt.

(K.)

14 Ed. III. stat. 1. c. 21.

ITEM, though the commons of the realm did pray the King, that he would, by assent of the Parliament, grant and establish, that never should be taken more custome of a sacke of wolle then halfe a mark, nor of leade nor tinne, lether nor wolfelles but the old custome; neverthelefs the King prayeth the prelates earles barons and all the commonaltie for the great busines which he hath now in hand, as they well know, that they would grant to him some aide upon the wolles lether wolfelles and other merchandizes, to endure for a small season: whereupon deliberation had, the said prelates earles barons and commons of his realme, hath granted to him forty shillings to be taken of every sacke of wooll, and forty shillings of every three hundred wolfelles,

and

and forty shillings of every last of lether and other merchandises that pass beyond the sea after the rate. And to begin at the feast of Easter in the fourteenth yeere of his raigne, and to endure till the feast of Pentecost then next following; and from that feast till the feast of Pentecost then next following into a yere. And for this grant the King, by the assent of the prelates earles barons and all other assembled in Parliament, hath granted, that from the feast of Pentecost which cometh into one yeere, he nor his heires shall not demand, assesse, nor take, *nor suffer to be taken*, more custome of a sacke of woolle of any Englishman, but halfe a marke onely. And upon the wolfelles and lether the olde custome. And the sacke ought to conteine twenty-six stones, and every stone fourteen Pounds.

(L.)

ROT. PARL. 17 ED. III. No. 28.

ITEM, q la maletoute des leynes se teigne a demy mark come en temps de ses progenitours ad este usez, & *p* estatut puis en vre temps grantee. Et çoment q les marchandz eient grantez par eux, sanz assent des communes, un subside XL S. de chescun sac de leyne outre la droiturele maletoute de demy mark, voillez s'il vous pleft aver regard,

q tut

q tut eſt en charge & a meſchief de voz communes. Par qoi cel meſchief, ſi vous pleſt, ne voillez ſoeffrir, mes ſoit amendez a ceſt Parlement : qar ce eſt encontre reſon, q la comune de lour biens ſoient p marchandz chargez.

Responſio—L'entente de nre ſeign' le Roi n'eſt pas de charger les comunes p le ſubſide q les marchandz lui ont grantez, n'en poet eſtre entenduz en charge des communes, noement deſicome les communes ont mys un certein pris ſur les leynes p my les counteez; lequel pris le Roi voet q eſtoiſe, & q dedeinz cel pris nulles leynes ſoient achatees, ſur forfaiture de meiſmes les leynes en les mayns des marchandz qi les iſſint achatent,

(M.)

ROT. PARL. 21 ED. III. No. 16.

ITEM, prie la commune, q lui pleiſe ſovenir, coment au Parlement tenuz cy l'an de ſon Regne XVII, & al drein Parlement cy tenuz devant ore, acordee & grante fut p nre dit ſeignr le Roi & ſon conſeil, qe pur les grantz charges q la comune ſoeffre & porte annuelment, come des quinziſmes, neofiſmes, & leines, mes ne duiſſent avoir curreu ne iſſeu commiſſion hors de la chauncellerie, come de hobeleries, archeries, priſes des vitailles, ne
auxint

auxint commiffions d'eftendre les terres des certeines gentz outre la fome de certeine value, ne de autres charges lever du poeple fi eles ne feuffent grantez en Parlement; lefqueux ordinances font de rien tenuz: Par quei le poeple eft tout enpoveri & anenti. De q nei ils prient a nre dit feignr le Roi, q li plefe pitee prendre de fon people, & les ordinances & graunts du Parliament fetz au people affermer & tenir. Et q fi tieles commiffions iffent fanz affent du Parlement, q gentz de commune q fe fentent grevez puiffent avoir brefs de furfeer la dite ordeinance, & q le poeple ne foit tenuz a celes obeier.

Refponfio.
Si nule tiele impofition fu faite, ele fu faite *p* grande neceffite, & ce de l'affent des prelatz, contes, barons, & autres grantz, & afcuns des comunes adonqs prefentz. Nientmeyns, nre feignr le Roi ne voet q tiele impofition noun duement foit 'tretee en confequence; einz voet q les ordeinances dont cefte petition fait mention foient bonement gardez. Et quant a les prifes des vitailles, fauvee totefoiz la prerogative nre feignr le Roi, fa volente eft, q gre foit fait a ceux defqueux eles font & ferront iffint prifes.

ROT.

(N.)

ROT. PARL. 25 ED. III. No. 22.

ITEM fuppliont la dite commune, q come les marchauntz eont grantez a nre feign' le Roi XL. S. de fac de Leyne, laquele chofe chiet en charge du poeple & nemy des 'marchauntz ; q'il plefe a nre dit feign' le Roi, pur relevement de fon people, q les ditz XL S. ne feont mes demaundez ne leeves deforenavant. Et q commiffions ne foent faites fur tieles grantes fingulers, s'il ne foit en plein Parlement. Et fi nul tiel grant foit fait hors du Parlement, foit tenuz pur nul : Qar *p* caufe des ditz XL S. les marchauntz achatent les Leynes *p* taunt le meyns, & les vendont a chier. Et q touz maners des marchauntz, fi bien povers come riches, & fi bien des aliens dome des ligeaunce nre feignr le Roi, forpris fes enemys, eont fraunche poer de paffer ove lour marchandifes, faunz eftre reftrent des marchauñtz q fe dient eftre marchauntz le Roi, ou *p* altre quecumq finguler, paiaunt au Roi ce q *ap*tent. Et en cas q il plefe a nre dit feignr le Roi, en cefte fa grante neceffite, la fubfid' de XL S. avant dit un di an ou un an avoir,

lui

lui plefe a les Piers & Commune de la terre fa volunte monftrer, en comfort de eaux.

Refponfio.—Por ce q le fubfid' fut grante a nre feign' le Roi pur grante neceffite, laquele uncore dure, & fe monftre plus grant de jour en autre; quele chofe monftre a les Grantz & Communes a ceo Parlement affemblez de p nre feignr le Roi, les ditz feignrs & communes de commune affent ont grante a mefme n're feign' le dit fubfid', a prendre de la fefte de Seint Michel prefchein a venir tan q a la fin de deux aunz prefcheins fuantz.

(O.)

ROT. PARL. 36 ED. III. No. 26.

Item fupplie fa dit commune, q come en ceft prefent Parlement il les bie de charger d'un grant fubfide pur un temps; quel ils font preftz & volentrifs granter, en confort de lui, eantz regarde a la grande neceffite q lour eft monftre de *pt.* fon confeil; iffint & en manere tiele, q'apres le dit terme rien ne foit pris ne demande de euz, forfpris foulement l'aunciene cuftume de demy Marc: ne q ceft grant ore fait, ou q'ad efte fait avant ces heures, ne foit treit en enfample ne charge du dit commune en temps a venir. Et q les marchantz denifzeins puiffent paffer ove lour

lour leines fi avant come les foreins faunz eftre reftreint. Et q nul fubfide, n'autre charge, foit mis ne grante fur les leines *p* les marchantz, ne *p* nul autre deforeenavant faunz affent du Parlement.

Refponfio.—Il pleft au Roi.

(P.)

ROT. PARL. 2 RICH. II. No. 30.

Item remonftrent les coes, coment ore tarde, puis la darrein confeil tenuz a Weftm', furent mandez diverfes lettres de credence deffouz le prive feal, par certains chivalers & efquiers de la courte le roi, es diverfes parties du Roialme, pur faire chevance d'argent a l'oeps le roi ; quelles lettres avoient les cowes blankes, & les ditz credenfours de lour auctoritee demefne efcriverent les nouns des plufours gentz fur les cowes des lettres fuis dites & baillerent a eux les lettres, affermantz q le roi les maunda a eux, & demanderent de eux grandes fommes tielles come lour pleuft, & ceux qui fe excuferent de les paier tielles fommes les manacerent fortement de *p* le roi, & les comanderent de *p* le roi d'eftre devant le confeil le roi, & affignerent a eux jours a leur volentee ; a grande damage & affraye des ditz povres coes, & *enfclandre du roi,* & *encontre la joye loye de la terre.* Par quoy fupplient les dites coes, q'ordene foit, q coment q'il plefe au roi d'envoier lettres pur apprompter argent en temps a venir, & celui a qi la lettre vient excufe refonablement du dit approinpt, q'il foit a ce receu, fanz lui mettre au travail, ou lui grever par fommons ou par autre manere.

Refponfio.—Il pleft au Roi.

(Q.)

1 RICH. III. CHAP. II.

The Subjects of this Realm fhall not be charged by any Benevolence, &c.

" The King remembering how the Commons
" of this his realm, by new and unlawful in-
" ventions and inordinate covetife, againft the
" law of this realm, have been put to great
" thraldom and importable charges and ex-
" actions, and in efpecial by a new impofition
" called *benevolence,* whereby divers years the
" fubjects and Commons of this land, againft
" their wills and freedoms, have paid great
" fums of money to their almoft utter de-
" ftruction: for divers and many worfhipful
" men of this realm, by occafion thereof, were
" compelled by neceffity to break up their
" houfe-

" households, and to live in great penury and
" wretchedness, their debts unpaid, and their
" children unpreferred; and such memorials as
" they had ordained to be done for the wealth
" of their souls, were anentized and annulled,
" to the great displeasure of God, and the de-
" struction of this realm :" Therefore the King
will it to be ordained, by the advice and assent of
of the Lords spiritual and temporal and the
Commons in this present Parliament assembled,
and by the authority of the same, that his subjects, and the commonalty of this his realm,
from henceforth in no wise be charged by none
such charge, exaction, or imposition, called a
benevolence, nor by such like charge; and that
such exactions, called *benevolences,* before this
time taken, be taken for no example to make
such or any like charge of any of his said subjects of this realm hereafter, but it shall be
damned and annulled for ever.

(R.)

11 HEN. VII. CAP. 10.

Praien the Commons in this present Parliament assembled, that where divers and many of
your subjects severally granted to your highnes
divers summes of money, *of their free wills and*
bene-

benevolence, for the defence of this your realme, toward the charge and great expences that your highneffe fufteined and bare for the faid defence, as well in your faid voiage royall in the parts of France beyond the fea, as on this fide, in for and about the fame, which voiage your faid highneffe tooke upon you in your moft royall perfon, to the great jeorperdy and labour of the fame, as well for the faid defence of this your faid realme, as for the furety, profite, weale and commoditie of us all, your true liege men and fubjects inhabited in the fame, of which fummes of money divers your faid fubjects full lovingly have made to you true paiment according to their graunts, and other many feveral fummes of money by divers of your fubjects to you in that party granted as yet remaine not content ne paied, part whereof refteth in the hands of the faid graunters, and part in the hands of the faid commiffioners, collectors, and receivors in that party affigned for the levy, rering and keeping of the fame, which is not onely to the damage, loffe and hurt of your faid highnes, but alfo to the murmur, grudge, and mifcontenting of fuch your faid fubjects as have made their faid paiments in that behalfe; wherefore may it pleafe your faid highnes, by the advife and affent of your Lords fpirituall and temporall, and the Commons in this prefent Parliament affembled, and by authoritie of the fame,

to

to ordaine, enact and establish, that proclamation be made in every shire, towne, and hundred, within this your realme, that every person and persons, which have not contented and paied the summes of money by them granted to your highnes for the causes remembred, that such commissioners, collectors, receivors, and other persons deputed to receive the same, doe make paiment thereof within three moneths next after the said proclamation made, to the said commissioners, collectors, receivors, or other persons that hereafter shall be thereunto deputed or assigned by your highnesse, and by your letters patents under your great seale in likewise to be proclaimed. And that the said commissioners have authoritie and power to make processe to take every such person or persons as so shall make default of paiment, by his body, and the same to commit to the common gaile, there to remaine and abide without baile or mainprise, to the time he hath paid his said duties, or else find sufficient surety for the paiement of the same to the said commissioners agreeable. And if any such person that hath not made paiment of this said duty graunted be deceased, that then the goods and cattels of him deceased, *being in the hands of his executors or administrators not administred*, be charged and chargeable to the said paiment. And that the said commissioners have like authoritie

and

and power, to doe ordaine, and award proceſſe for the levie of the ſame, as the barons of the King's exchequer doe and may doe for the King's duties reſting afore them of record in the ſaid exchequer. And the ſaid commiſſioners, collectors, or receivors, afore this time thereunto deputed, or that heereafter for and to the ſame ſhall be deputed, having and taking the receite of the ſame your money, or any parcel thereof, be ſeverally countable for the portions by them ſeverally received, before your treaſurer of your warres that was by you aſſigned in your ſaid voiage roiall, or any other perſon or perſons that heereafter by your highneſſe ſhall be thereunto deputed and aſſigned, of and for all ſuch ſummes of money as they ſeverally have received, or ſhall receive, or that ſeverally ſhall come to their hands, before ſuch auditors as by your highnes ſhall be aſſigned in that part. And if any of the ſaid commiſſioners, collectors, or receivors, come not to make their accounts at ſuch day and place as ſhall be limited in your privie ſeale to them directed in that party, that then upon certificate of the delivery of the ſaid writs or privie ſeales made by him, that the ſame delivered upon his oath unto the chauncellor of England for the time being, the ſaid chauncellor for the ſame time being hath authoritie and power to make commiſſions under your great ſeale,

seale, to certaine perfons by his difcretion to be limited and choofen, to take the bodies of the faid perfons that fo fhall make default, and them to commit to ward (unleffe then he make before the faid treafurer, or commiffioners, fuch excufe as to them fhall feeme reafonable), there to remaine till they have made their accounts of and for the premiffes, and fatisfied, contented, and paied the duty by them due upon their faid accounts, unto your faid treafurer of your Warres, or to fuch other perfon or perfons to your ufe, as your grace fhall depute and affigne in that party to receive the fame. And over this be it enacted by the faid authoritie, that if any travers fortune to be betweene the faid commiffioners afore this time affigned to receive the King's faid duties, collectors, and the faid grantors, of and for paying and not paying, receiving or not receiving of the faid fumme or fummes of money, or any part thereof; that then if the faide grauntors fhewe acquittance, writing, bill or billets, whereby it may appeare afore the commiffioners hereafter to be affigned, that the faid commiffioners or collectors afore this time affigned in forme rehearfed, have received the fumme or fummes of money, or any part thereof, that fhall be in travers, or that the faid grauntors offer to bring two witneffes or mo, that will witneffe and teftifie the faid paiment; or that any grauntor or

grauntors

grauntors denie the graunt of any such summe or summes of money, or any part thereof of them demaunded; that thereupon the said commissioners heereafter to be assigned, have authoritee and power to heare the whole matter, evidence, writings, witnesse, and proofes, concerning the said travers, and denying of the said graunts, and then to charge and discharge every of the said persons by their discretions, as they shall seeme best; and the same charge or discharge to bind and discharge every of the said parties against the King's highnes, as if it were adjudged before the auditors assigned by due originall in any of the King's courts of record between party and party in actions of account, or else that the King were plaintiffe in the said action of account. Be it also ordained by the said authoritie, that the said commissioners heereafter to be assigned by the King's highnesse, shall, by their discretion upon their account and full paiment made of all summes of money by them received or to be received by the collector or receivers of the said summes of benevolence, allowe unto the said receivers and collectors such their reasonable costs and rewards, as they for the gathering of the said summes have sustained. Provided alway, that this act shall not extend to charge any heire of any

Q.   man

man that hath afore time granted any summe of money by way of his benevolence.

(S.)

13 CHA. II. CH. 4.

We your Majesties most loyal and obedient subjects, the Lords and Commons in Parliament assembled, taking into confideration your Majesty's great and important occasions for a speedy supply of monies, which can noe waies be so reddyly raised as by a free and voluntary present to your Majesty from those who are able and willing to aide your Majesty in this suddaine exigency, as a testimony of their affections to your Majesty, and in case of the poorer sort of your subjects, doe therefore beseech your Majesty, that it may be enacted, and be it enacted by the King's most excellent Majesty, by and with the advice and consent of the Lords and Commons in this present Parliament assembled, and by the authority of the same, that your Majesty may issue out such and so many several commissions under your Majesty's great seal of England into the several counties, cities, towns corporate, and all other places in England and Wales, and town of Berwick upon Tweed, directed to such persons as your Majesty shall think fit, for the receiving of such subscriptions as your

Majesty's

Majesty's good subjects shall voluntarily offer for supply of your Majesty's pressing occasions; and, likewise to issue such other commissions to such other persons as your Majesty shall think fit, for collecting and receiving the monies so subscribed; the acquittances of which respective receivers, or of any one of them, are immediately to be made and given without any fee, upon payment made, and shall be an absolute discharge for the sum so subscribed; and in case such subscriptions shall, upon any occasion, be returned into the court of exchequer, or any other place, the payment thereof shall be likewise returned together with the same. Provided that no process shall issue out of the exchequer against any person so subscribing, but within two years next after the passing of this act. And for the better execution of the said service, the said commissioners of the counties, cities, towns corporate, and all other places aforesaid, respectively shall, and are hereby enjoined, with all convenient speed after the issuing out and receite of the said respective commissions, to meet together at the most usual and common place of meeting, within each of the said counties, cities, towns corporate, and all other places; and the said commissioners, or so many of them as shall be present at the said first general meeting, or the major part of them, may, by them, by their consents and agreements, sever themselves into hundreds, rapes, wapentakes, wardes, and

and other places within their refpective limitts, in fuch manner and forme as to them fhall feeme expedient; and fhall likewife, from tyme to tyme, give notice of the refpective tymes and places of their meetings, to the end that any perfons, bodies politick, or corporate, may, if they pleafe, refort to them, and make fuch offers or prefent to your Majefty, as their own hearts fhall prompt them to.

Provided always, that no perfon, not being a peere of this realme, fhall, in fuch offer or prefent to your Majeftie, exceed the fume of 200l. nor any peere of this realme the fume of 400l. Provided alfo, that no commiffions to be iffued out by virtue of this act, fhall be of force or continue as to the receiving of any monies, or fubfcriptions for monies, after the feaft of St. John the Baptift, which fhall be in the year of our Lord one thoufand fix hundred and fixty-two. And be it hereby declared, that no commiffions or aides of this nature can be iffued out, or levied, but by authority of parliament; and that this act, and the fupply hereby granted, fhall not be drawne into example for the tyme to come.

This ftatute is recited in Pulton's ftatutes. Edit. an. 1661. There is alfo a copy in Debrett's Parliamentary Regifter of 1778, Vol. 10. of that feffion.

F I N I S.

www.ingramcontent.com/pod-product-compliance
Lightning Source LLC
Chambersburg PA
CBHW021942160426
43195CB00011B/1189